William B. Jordan, Jr.
10) '97

Grave Matters

Other books by the author

The Innocent Anthropologist
A Plague of Caterpillars
Not a Hazardous Sport
The Coast
The Duke of Puddledock: In the Footsteps of Stamford Raffles
Smashing Pots: Feats of Clay from Africa

Grave Matters

A Lively

History

of Death

Around the

World

NIGEL BARLEY

A John Macrae Book
HENRY HOLT AND COMPANY NEW YORK

For Din

So long as men can breathe or eyes can see,
So long lives this and this gives to life to thee.

Henry Holt and Company, Inc.
Publishers since 1866
115 West 18th Street
New York, New York 10011

Henry Holt® is a registered trademark
of Henry Holt and Company, Inc.

Library of Congress Cataloging-in-Publication Data
Barley, Nigel.
[Dancing on the grave]
Grave matters: a lively history of death around the world
Nigel Barley.—1st American ed.
p.   cm.
Originally published: Dancing on the grave.
Great Britain: J. Murray.
"A John Macrae book."

ISBN 0-8050-4824-3

Includes bibliographical references and index.
1. Funeral rites and ceremonies—Cross-cultural studies.
2. Death—Social aspects—Cross-cultural studies.   I. Title.
GT3150.B34   1997   97-19052
393—dc21   CIP

Henry Holt books are available for special promotions and
premiums. For details contact: Director, Special Markets.

First published in the United States in 1997
by Henry Holt and Company, Inc.

Originally published in Great Britain by John Murray
(Publishers) Ltd. under the title *Dancing on the Grave*

First American Edition 1997

A John Macrae Book

Printed in the United States of America
All first editions are printed on acid-free paper.∞

2   4   6   8   10   9   7   5   3   1

Contents

Introduction

There is a general expectation that nonfiction books will tell you how to be perfect and live forever, or, at the very least, how to cook flawless bouillabaisse or build a set of practical pine bookshelves. Alas, this is not such a book. Examination of the deathways of other peoples seems to dismantle many of the certainties we feel about mortality without offering a single glib solution to the problem of death. Different cultures have located this problem in quite different places, for everywhere death is part of a wider vision of life, so that what is supposed to be a window on eternity becomes a mirror in which we see ourselves. For the West the problem of death centers on maintaining individual existence beyond the grave, for Buddhists it is a matter of getting rid of individual existence, for the headhunters of South America the problem is one of reassigning it, and for many Africans it is one of dismantling existence and recycling its various components.

Having stripped death of many of its cosmological components, Western culture frequently views death as a social worker's problem that requires emotional counselling. Elsewhere it may be felt that the required training is rather in how to kill others magnificently.

When discussing this book, I found many people assumed that, as an anthropologist, I would conclude the West has got death all wrong and that the Bong-Bongo, or whoever, have got it properly sorted out. There was a belief that there must be a simple off-the-peg ritual we can bolt on to make death 'all right' and turn its sting into a kiss. But every view of death generates its own problem, one that often seems to have been deliberately set up in order to be insoluble, so the primary value of studying other views of death is, perhaps, to learn how little of our own view is given by Nature. We could change if we wanted to—but we do have to want to. To counsel others on such matters requires great wisdom, humanity and judgement and these are not part of any recognized academic discipline—least of all anthropology. Anthropologists know a little about how some peoples see death, but they know nothing of how they *should* see it and it is inappropriate for them to adopt the missionary position by assuming other cultures have got it right.

Yet if the road to Hell is paved with good intentions, the road to Death is paved with platitudes. Many of the rites of death, when translated—as Westerners like to do—into 'beliefs,' turn out to be warm-and-serve truisms about life and death being but twin faces of the same reality. Animals and plants die to give us life. The old die to make room for the young. Animal death promotes plant growth. One season's crop of plants carries the seeds for the next—and so on. Death is Janus-faced. As Levi-Strauss pointed out concerning myth, it is impossible to exaggerate the poverty of basic ideas on which such edifices of faith are based. Yet interest in 'belief' may simply be a largely Western obsession. In China great concern with a common ritual response has coexisted quite happily with an overwhelming disregard for similarity of belief so it does not matter very much what you claim to think you are doing as long as you do it like everyone else. It is left to a small number of foreign and local experts to worry about ideas.

On this most unpromising basis, different people have raised up complex and tortuous rites that are elaborated into true works of art. Monuments to the dead are also monuments to Man's ingenuity and they enter definitively into our notions of common humanity. Some cultures, most famously Ancient Egypt, have virtually bankrupted themselves to deal adequately with the death of a single person while others, such as the nomadic peoples of southern

Africa, have done little more than pull down the roof onto the corpse and walk away. This is not solely a matter of relative wealth or technological complexity. In the most difficult environmental conditions, Australian peoples have developed complicated funeral practices that have entered largely into the grander theories of the human sciences. Various explanations have been advanced for disengagement with the dead—a more general lack of concern with time depth, lack of agricultural models of recycling fertility or role constancy, a vision of the world that does not see life as a limited and finite good, the replacement of wealth in human beings by the notion of capital. Sometimes these depend on environmental or economic underpinnings. All will take you a certain distance but, like most anthropological theories, they are a loose garment that fits where it touches. Examined closely, they are either downright false or simply tautological. There is no single explanation of one society's concern with death and another's neglect of it. We cannot define death out of existence as a mere sociological epiphenomenon.

Where does a book like this come from? In the course of writing such a work, many forgotten memories surface. Perhaps it goes back to my first encounter with death as a child. A neighbor had died, leaving his young widow. She was a member of a cooperative store where the customers shared profits at the end of each year. They also arranged funerals. This was a matter of great scandal. "Sharing in the profits of your own husband's funeral," tutted one old lady. "It's disgusting. It's just like cannibalism!" The word was new to me. I had to ask for it to be explained. Perhaps this book is a continuation of the search for that explanation.

1

The Universality of Death

'We're all in this thing alone'
Lily Tomlin

It is not easy to be interested in death. Concern with the way of mortality is 'morbid', worse 'sick'. In Africa, my constant presence at funerals was rapidly noted. 'You are like a vulture,' one man remarked coolly. 'I see you climbing the hills and I know someone else must have gone.' A more politicized view would seize on this as a marker of the predatory nature of all research or the role of the anthropologist as undertaker and embalmer of moribund cultures. In Java, requests to look at the cemetery are taken even more seriously, for you do not seek out the dead without due cause. 'You cannot go to a cemetery,' said my shocked host. 'I cannot take you. People would see us. They would think we were mad, witches looking for fresh corpses to eat.'

Yet death is more than a merely individual experience and anthropologists have worked hard to give it a big part in the collective drama of life. Anthropological pioneers such as Bronislaw Malinowski saw it as the origin of all religion but then the lines he drew between magic, science and religion made this self-confirming. Subsequent writers have seen the fear and denial of death as the origin of *all* culture.* The emptiness of such positions

---

*Baumann, 1993

is not that they explain too little but – like all psychoanalysis – too much.

Archaeologists have similarly been good press agents for death. In the archaeological record, ritual concern with mortal remains is amongst the first signposts that Man has evolved from mere hominoid and emerged as a higher being. One of the ironies of this is that such 'ritual concern' can look just like the physical interference with remains that comes from being eaten by fellow higher beings. 'Ritual concern' shows intellect and respect but cannibalism – it is assumed – is a mark of gross animality. Death always seems to wear two faces, to be inherently and usefully ambiguous and it is principally paradox, not horror, that stalks the Valley of the Shadow of Death. So when Peking Man split open human long bones and crania in 400,000 BC should we see him as practising ennobling funerary ritual or primitive cannibalism? They are, of course, the same thing. Once the line to humanity has been crossed, eating the dead is as much a ritual act as burying them, for both – like the Javanese fear of hungry witches – are merely different cultural ways of dealing with the problem that fellow humans are made of meat.

Aristotle saw humour as the primary distinguishing feature of humanity, others have homed in on the possession of language. Voltaire said with greater truth that humans are the only creatures that know they are going to die. Death sits as a sort of boundary, a collective headstone and footstone, marking off and defining both ends of the human condition.

Researchers on animal communication have scored a recent breakthrough. Opposing the idea that only humans have language ability they taught chimpanzees to use human deaf and dumb signing. Then, inevitably, they went one better and sought to destroy the next barrier artificially dividing man from beast. A researcher had to inform Washoe, most famous of the signing chimpanzees, that her baby was dead and tried to get this across by joining together the signs 'baby' and 'finish'. What Washoe can really have made of this we will never know, but when asked the

14

chimpanzee's reaction, the researcher made his whole body go slack and looked infinitely depressed. A man apes a chimp and so sustains the argument that chimps are like men and, having similar knowledge of death, have similar rights in life.

One mainstream of early anthropology such as that of Levi-Bruhl and Evans-Pritchard centred debates about the psychic unity of mankind on the logical processes of reasoning. How was it that different peoples, faced with the same evidence, reached entirely different conclusions? Did Primitive Man have a genetically different mind/brain? Were different logical processes involved in different mind-sets or was it all merely a matter of different cultural presuppositions that set what was basically the same instrument playing different tunes? The cosy consensus reached – despite spirited later challenges – is that all men think the same. This has now been inscribed in the founding assumptions of anthropology as an unchallengeable moral fact. To oppose it is to be a racist, probably a wicked person and certainly a bad anthropologist.

Yet, there is a sense in which the man in the street has bypassed this debate and staked out the ground with different moral markers by perversely homing in not on the rational but the emotional universality of Man. This is an approach that has a certain academic respectability and even greater human appeal. After a day eliciting recondite and unconvincing explanations from local people at an Indonesian funeral, building a rickety bridge to human understanding, nothing conveys a greater certainty of real mutual comprehension than catching a villager's eye as the beautifully dressed high priest trips and sprawls full-length in the mud and you all explode in laughter. Then, for the first time all day, you *know* you have understood each other. This empathetic view finds its commonest expression in popular TV programmes of soft-core ethnographic content. These reduce to the po-faced statement: 'Life consists of birth, growing-up, marriage, parenting and death with an awful lot of suffering in between. This is the Universal Human Experience. To overcome suffering and smile nobly through the tears is the Universal Lot of Man.'

Judgements of universality are now made by the mass media rather than anthropologists – much to their disgust – and to deny the emotional universality of death is to argue against being moved by the filmed sobs of a famine victim's widow. It is to drive a sceptical wedge between the mourners round a Soweto grave and the distant viewer. It is to devalue sympathy in general. In line with our own preconceptions, Westerners characterize mourning as not a ritual, social or physical state but one of disordered emotions that may require therapy. Yet anthropologists have maintained that the dominant emotion at Chinese funerals may not be grief but scarcely concealed fear of the contagion of death.* In many of the cultures where people are held to have been killed by spiteful human action in the form of witchcraft and sorcery, outrage may be the dominant feeling. Different sexes may be expected to react in different ways, men with anger, women with tears.

Doubts about the matter were apparently compromised once and for all – again by television – during the Vietnam War. The voice of General Westmorland, delivering the anthropologically somewhat undeveloped statement, 'The Oriental doesn't put the same high price on life as the Westerner,' was broadcast over a picture of an old Vietnamese lady trembling to the point of collapse as a muscular Western hand thrust an M-16 carbine hard against her head. Put in this form, the anti-relativist argument is hard to oppose.

Yet anyone who has worked amongst an alien people knows that we can never know what another individual 'feels', let alone a whole people. Some cultures seem to highlight emotions that to us are unimportant – like the *amae*, 'dependency', that seems central to understanding much of Japanese interaction and neurosis. Or whole emotions can disappear, like the *asidie* of Renaissance man. The subject has been unhelpfully complicated by philosophers who have turned the matter into a problem of language and simply analysed the language of emotion. It is of no value to us to learn that when one says, 'I'm afraid I can't see you,' that the

*Watson and Rawski, 1988:121

speaker does not actually *feel* fear. Nor does it help us much to know that Ilongot words for 'anger' and 'passion' refer not to internal states but rather to forms of social action and discourse. It is only the false hope of directly comparing inner states that makes the question of emotion of interest in the first place because it involves, for us, the ultimate definition of a universal humanity.

———

As a child I was much impressed by a woman in our village who wore a black armband when one of the Archers died. Extending the mourning to her dog, she had a special black leather lead that was used as a substitute for the normal brown one. On these occasions, her whole demeanour was one of such profound sorrow that there seems little reason to assume that it was not deeply felt. One does not need to have actually existed to be mourned. It is nowadays a common phenomenon for television stations to be overwhelmed by expressions of grief whenever they 'kill off' a popular character in a soap opera. Wreaths arrive, together with letters of reproach, tearful telephone calls, even accusations of murder and death threats for the producer. Quality newspapers rejoice in such irrationality as showing how many lunatics there are about. Hack psychologists suck on their pipes and write columns diagnosing such fans as unable to distinguish fantasy from reality. Sociologists intuit that mourning fans are a powerful symptom of the decay of society in that shadows on a screen have become more important than flesh and blood neighbours. Postmodernists read the fans as heroes who gloriously celebrate the inauthenticity of representations.

Perhaps we should see these fictitious dead as just the opposite of those real babies whose tragic deaths tear no larger hole in the social fabric and are therefore ignored by all but the immediate family. The screen dead have an existence that is purely social and consensual. After all, the criterion of fame is that one is violently loved or hated by people one has never even met and nowadays stars do not have to exist any more to continue to perform. When the actor, Brandon Lee, was accidentally shot during the making of the film *The Crow*, images of him were electronically reprocessed so that he could continue to play his role in subsequent scenes. It is quite normal, when stars themselves die, for them to be mourned rather as characters than as actors, the body itself being something of a tangential embarrassment in that it contradicts the edited, intensified reality of the screen image.

A case in point is the account of the death of the Mexican film actress, Lupe Velez, who killed herself with sleeping pills in 1944. In preparation, she put on her best silver lamé gown, filled the room with flowers and perfumed candles and composed herself on the bed with hands piously clasped as though in prayer. In the night, however, the emetic effect of the pills took hold so that *in extremis* she rushed to the bathroom, tripped and fell. Her maid found her the next morning, stone dead, bare rump erect, head plunged into the lavatory bowl and kneeling in a pool of vomit and excrement.

Since this was not an acceptable death for a film star, the facts were concealed. The original 'Sleeping Beauty' version, as planned by Lupe herself, was fed to the press. Death – like Life – follows Art.

We can never be sure what counts as an 'emotion' as opposed to a purely physical response; terms like 'tiredness', 'disgust' and 'grief' seem to dissolve when we look at them. Much of the effort of Western psychology has been aimed at reclassifying all reactions as either profoundly internal/emotional or purely external/responsive. Yet Indonesians doggedly maintain that they feel both in their livers. Working with the emotion words of other cultures is like trying to translate smells.

'This war dance (*ukukina*),' said an old Nyakyusa man, 'is mourning, we are mourning the dead man. We dance because there is war in our hearts. A passion of grief and fear exasperates us (*ilyojo likutusila*).' Since this statement is the clue both to the present and to the traditional meaning of the war dance to the chief mourners, we must examine the language carefully. *Elyojo* means a passion of grief, anger or fear; *ukusila* means to annoy or exasperate beyond endurance. In explaining *ukusila* one man put it like this: 'If a man continually insults me then he exasperates me (*ikusila*) so that I want to fight him.' Death is a fearful and grievous event that exasperates those men most nearly concerned and makes them want to fight. The chief mourners and personal friends among the women assuage their feelings in a ceremonial wailing, among the men in the ceremonial war dance. 'A kinsman when he dances assuages his passionate grief (*ilyojo*); he goes into the house to weep and then he comes out and dances the war dance; his passionate grief is made tolerable in the dance (lit. "he is able to endure it there, in the dance"), it bound his heart and the dance assuages it.'*

Fine, but for all their tortured straining, Godfrey Wilson's explanations leave you rather less sure than before that you know what was going on in people's hearts and minds. An obvious solution is to short-circuit the proceeding by looking not at what people *say* but what they *do*, showing all the Westerner's naïve trust in external reality. Human beings cry and wail when they are sad. We assume we can recognize this as a universal language of grief when we see it. So does everyone cry and wail at funerals? Is this the sign of a common emotional bedrock?

Often tears are the least of it, the calm beneath the storm. In some parts of Africa, funerals may end in fights in which people are killed; death seems to feed on itself. In Tonga, people formerly chopped off their fingers. Among the Ojibwa of Canada mourning was similarly extreme with men, women and children pouring ashes over their heads. Men alone, it seems, went further and pushed knives, needles and thorns through the skin of the chest and arms. A description of the Australian Warramungas' reaction to death has become something of a classic:

*Wilson, 1939:13.

Late one afternoon, just before sunset, and immediately after the performance of several sacred ceremonies, we were all leaving the corrobboree ground when a sudden loud piercing wail broke out in the direction of the man's camp. Every one knew that this meant that the man was dead or dying, and with one accord all the men, including the decorated performers, ran pell-mell, as hard as they could, towards the camp, most of them at the same time beginning to howl ... Some of the women, according to custom, had thrown themselves prostrate on the body, while others were standing or kneeling about, digging the sharp ends of fighting clubs and yam sticks into the crown of their heads, from which the blood streamed down their faces. All of them were howling and wailing at the top of their voices ... One man had been to his camp for a stone knife, and now rushed up yelling and brandishing his knife in the air. Suddenly he jumped into the group of men, gashed both his thighs deeply, cutting right across the muscles, and, unable to stand, fell down into the middle of the group, from which he was dragged after a time by three or four female relatives – his mother, wife and sisters – who immediately applied their mouths to the gaping wounds, while he lay exhausted on the ground ... The etiquette of mourning is elaborate, and the omission to do what was proper would indicate a want of respect which would be much resented by the dead man's spirit. On the camping ground several men were lying *hors de combat* with gashed thighs. They had done their duty and henceforth in token of this would be marked with deep scars. On one of these men we counted no fewer than twenty-six such scars ... The leg of the man who had most deeply gashed himself was held by his father, who, in turn, was embraced from behind by an aged man – the father-in-law of the patient - as if to support him in his grief. Sundry other men came up, one after the other, and there was a succession of embracings, accompanied by alternate howling and moaning.*

Such loud public grief fits all too easily into cosy Western assumptions that other peoples are less controlled than ourselves – 'closer to nature' – or more given to distasteful ostentation. Yet at Malay and Javanese funerals it is absolutely forbidden to cry as this

*Spencer and Gillen, 1912:426

would burden the departed. Never mind. In the 'heads-I-win-tails-you-lose' world where live our attitudes to cultural difference, we can still enshrine our own reasonableness as a universal yardstick. All we have to do is see Malays as 'slaves to custom' in a way quite unlike our natural selves. At Jewish funerals there seems to be an attempt to have it both ways with lavishly orchestrated mourning but with the photos of the deceased covered 'so he does not see our tears.'

But even so, surely it is not legitimate to simply note down these usages as different but accurate readings from a common thermometer of grief – with a small allowance made for each culture setting the thermostat a little higher or lower. This is like calling both face-slapping and dropping napalm sticks 'aggression'.

In a comic sketch, Bill Cosby tellingly contrasts black and white funerals in contemporary America. At the black funeral people fling themselves screaming on the coffin. At the white, a patrician voice merely asks, 'Excuse me. But is that dirt *strictly* necessary?' What both American repertoires have in common is the notion that funerals are about expressing the *emotional* links between the living and the dead, be they of respect or grief. Such actions are not, as is elsewhere the case, expected to affect the actual fate of the dead. Other peoples are unspeakably shocked that we hand over the bodies of our dead to complete strangers to strip, eviscerate and do with as they will. We in turn are scandalized by the employment of paid mourners who simulate pain. As Montaigne pointed out, 'Each man calls barbarism whatever is not his own practice.'

It is not just death itself that may be formally mourned.

> When the tooth of a chief falls, the wail of a dirge is raised by his family, an oven is kindled and sons gash their foreheads in mourning – this is a conventional tribute of affection to the ageing man for the food that he will now be unable to consume.*

*Firth, 1936:185

21

So sometimes those little anticipatory tastes of death, the fortieth birthday, the loss of physical or sexual powers, may also have to be culturally marked. Just think of the fun we could have charting our own decline instead of concealing it.

While the dominant model for the mind is now the computer, thanks to Freud we are still saddled with a model of human emotion from the age of the steam engine. Feelings are naturally in there, boiling away under pressure, trying to escape, needing outlets, though often bottled up by society. Weeping is a safety valve, a way of carefully 'letting off steam' that avoids a damaging explosion. Once pressure has been released, grief can be channelled and stilled.

Yet just as often, emotional display is required and has little to do with actual feelings, a socially demanded performance. Thus, the Spencer and Gillen passage about the Warramunga of Australia continues:

> Most of this was merely a matter of etiquette, and had no reference to any genuine feeling of regret. If a man, who stands in a particular relationship to you, happens to die, you must do the proper thing, which may be either gashing your thigh or cutting your hair, quite regardless of whether you were personally acquainted with the dead man or whether he was your dearest friend or greatest enemy.*

It is significant, after all, that Warramunga 'grief' makes a man slash his thighs for his mother's brother but burn his abdomen for his mother, while only *male* Ojibwa grief leads to skin-piercing. Grief is a final performance and, even where it is both felt and expressed, culture stands between us and the brute facts.

The actor Sir John Gielgud has a party trick of which interviewers never tire. He can cry at will, just sit down, open the lacrimous ducts and let 'spontaneous' tears flow down his cheeks. In this he is not alone. As late as the eighteenth century public

*Spencer and Gillen, 1912:429

lamentation with tears was still the rule in parts of rural Europe. And many peoples around the world such as – famously – the Andamanese execute the Gielgud trick as a standard mark of politeness.

Such performance may have great survival value. The failure to mourn is likely to reap the accusation that you were responsible for the death through witchcraft. A Trobriand leader may silently claim the death of an opponent by simply dressing up at the news instead of wearing mourning clothes.

A spouse's virtue will often be judged by the performance of mourning that is its public face. Among the Alaskan Tlingit the black paint of a widow's make-up would be examined by her dead husband's family to see that it was suitably tear-streaked. Failure to mourn properly might bring subtle or blatant public disgrace. In the late nineteenth century one widow was found not to have observed the rules, indeed to have so far disregarded them as to have an affair with a white man. At the final memorial festival to the husband, to ensure her public disgrace, his family sent out a boy, dressed in European clothes, to loudly play the squeeze-box.*

—*ove*—

'The Faces of Death, that's what you should watch.' A Malaysian museum colleague at one of those ideas-swapping sessions that tend to come late at night in the nearness of bars. He's doing 'adultery' – strong stuff in a Muslim state. I'm doing 'death.'

'The Faces of Death, what is it?'

He shrugs and makes a face. 'Newsreel footage. Different sorts of funerals around the world, some stuff in a morgue. Lots of people crying and carrying on, making sacrifices. *Kuru*, you know, that disease you get in New Guinea from eating people. I forget. I'll send it to you.' But when he sends me *The Faces of Death*, it's

*Olson, 1967:66

confiscated by H.M. Customs. 'Footage of the death and mutilation of humans and animals in various circumstances,' says the letter censoriously, 'judged by the intercepting officer to be obscene and therefore liable to seizure.'

A Muslim *kenduri* – prayers to ease the passage of a dead person's soul – in a Singapore highrise block. The shoes are spread in a fan around the door, as if at an exhibition of the social concomitants of footwear. There are women's shoes, tiny children's, men's slip-ons with the backs squashed comfily down, the neighbours' scuffed sandals, a teenager's fashionable Doc Marten's, doubly inconvenient in a culture where you have to be shod and unshod a dozen times a day to enter and leave a house. As I undo Western laces, I remember a joke told me by a Javanese imam: 'Why do we not have complicated songs and processions in the mosques like the Christians do in their churches? You don't know? Haven't you seen all those sandals by the door? It is because we have to put all our effort into making sure we leave with the same pair we arrived in.'

Inside, mourners are in traditional clothing or some sort of a compromise between that and normal clothes. Most of the men have *songkok* hats and sarongs, the little boys arrayed proudly in full Malay dress. The men are leading the prayers, the women grouped slightly to one side. Women should not have too much to do with death.

Two things strike a Westerner. First, it is all so relaxed, a family affair, no religious officials. Anyone who knows the prayers can do it. But a *wicked* man – they stress – would not know how. A mother dandles a baby as she chants, a boy taps out the rhythm gently with one finger on the top of his tiny cousin's head. Second, there are no tears. That would be a burden on the dead. They smile in greeting or flash eyebrow-raised hellos.

Afterwards, we eat and gossip. In an easy transition, the television is switched on lest we miss the football, Singapore versus Brunei. The women eat after the men.

'In England it is ladies first.'

'Well . . . that is what we *say*.'

Over the food, we discuss our various new infirmities and financial griefs since our last meeting. They ask about the book they know I'm writing on death and tell me about *kenduris* and how they have changed. 'The important thing,' says one like the school swot, 'is to know the right answers to the angel of death's questions when he cross-examines you after death. We learn that as children – like how to write a CV.'

In return I tell them about English funerals and mourning, how it is nowadays different from when I was a boy. Then we used to doff our hats to the war memorial and cover up mirrors when in mourning. 'Wah, they made us do that in the village when there was a thunderstorm. People do crazy things. Why do we do these things?'

The football finishes and an old film comes on, wailing violins, the Malay with Indonesian inflections just as they once spoke British English on the Broadway stage. We settle to watch. It will be an old legend from around the archipelago, sternly muscular and noble men betrayed by unworthy women, many tears, cursing, forgiveness, perhaps even a ghost. Shakespeare would have fitted right in here. The film starts with a village *kenduri*, men in fancy head-dresses, armed with daggers, traditional music. We laugh, recognizing ourselves as a pale shadow of these flickering images in black and white.

'Look,' I say provocatively. '*Real* Malays.'

They think about that. 'No,' says one at last, '*old* Malays. Please, we switch channel. There's basketball on.'

'Uncle,' whispers one of the boys. 'Come and watch my video. It's very good, very interesting – educational. It makes me want to be a doctor when I leave school.'

'Pornography,' I think, imagining panned vistas of slick Swedish flesh, throbbing bodily functions to a soundtrack of gasps and grunts. How shall I behave? As unshockably brazen – because godless – a Westerner? Yet how embarrassing. It is, of course, *The Faces of Death*. No problem, as a Westerner I know much more about the modalities of violent slaying and mayhem than about decent death.

25

Anthropologists have used the grief of funerals to play all sorts of games that stress the bridge between the individual and the communal. Durkheim saw grieving as strengthening social bonds by obliging large numbers of people to share and show emotions they might not naturally feel. For Radcliffe-Brown, weeping at funerals and elsewhere was a way of marking socially important links and the reliance of the one on the group. By the death of one, the whole group was threatened and huddled round to show and feel social solidarity. Following St Augustin, he saw mortuary rites as more for the benefit of the living than the dead. Moreover — and this was the insidiously clever part — people did not cry because they were sad. Rather, they were sad *because they cried*. The distinction is vital. After all, for most Westerners, the problem of grief is seen as that of getting the grief *out*, like lancing a boil. Nowadays, those who refuse to do so after some major disaster are likely to be harassed by outraged counsellors who see them as 'in denial'. For anthropologists, the problem is just the reverse. It is that of getting the grief *in*, being made to feel the way you ought.

No idea is too trivial to be invoked to explain human ritual. With a truly psychoanalytic lack of embarrassment Thomas Scheff reduces all mortuary ritual to a bloated cultural version of the infant game of 'peekaboo', where a mother covers her face with her hands and then suddenly reveals it again to her infant, crying 'Boo' — with its switching from loss, to denial of loss, to catharsis.* More interestingly, Hitchcock saw this game as the origin of the thriller.

In the West, mourning is nowadays viewed as a 'private' thing. The family always request 'to be left to their grief'. Public mourn-

*Scheff, 1977

26

ing immediately smacks of overblown hypocrisy. Show it and you don't mean it. Curiously, this is at variance with our approach to funerals as theatre. Like films and plays, funerals now have directors too. In undertaking establishments, an iron distinction is made between front and back, just like that between on- and off-stage, the part the public can see and that absolutely off limits. Yet, at funerals, the rule is that nowadays we must all be method actors, really feeling our mumbled lines. Anthropologists have looked primarily at ritualized public mourning in other cultures, treated it as if it were the entire mourning practice, and worried endlessly about whether the emotions expressed there are 'real'. As far as the 'in-out controversy' of emotions is concerned, it may be that the feelings of those at the periphery of social relations are intensified by ritual, those centrally affected reduced. No single model captures the whole picture.

It might seem inevitable that death would lead people around the world to question the relations of the temporary to the eternal, the public to the private, one generation to another and the relation of individual to the larger whole. According to anthropologists, these are indeed the very questions posed. Since they are the basic questions of Western sociology, however, we may well be permitted to doubt the objectivity of such a happy coincidence. It is more accurate to say that notions of what it means to be dead are always part of a more general idea of what it means to be a living human being in the first place and funerary behaviour and beliefs around the world read like an extended discussion of the notion of the person.

The Melanesian Dobu have their own view of the relations between mourning and grief. Radcliffe-Brown-like they see death as *caused by* mourning:

> Sinebomatu, the woman of the north-east wind, went to bathe with her granddaughter. The grandmother went seawards down a stream. She peeled her skin off and threw it away. She came inland to her granddaughter. Her granddaughter wailed crying: 'My grandmother

is an old woman. You aren't her.' She replied, 'No. I *am* your grand-mother.'

'You're lying. You're a different woman. My grandmother's an old woman.'

She replied, 'You're wailing. I'll fetch my skin.'

She fetched her skin and put it on again like a shirt. She came back. She said, 'You wailed. I've brought my skin. If you hadn't wailed and we had gone back to the village you could have changed your wrin-kled skin when you got old.'

The snake, monitor lizard, crab and lobster ate a part of her skin. They shed their old skins and live for ever. We die.*

The Nigerian Nupe have a similar story. God inaugurated death because men started carrying tree trunks around, mourning and giving them funerals. Like many a parent since, slapping a whinge-ing child, God gave them death, gave them something to cry for.

Even were we able to isolate one specific private, therefore – we might hope – involuntary gesture, this would be no infallible help in the understanding of the emotional response to death across cultures. Tears are not shed just for sadness. It is rather that any excess of emotion can end in tears. As the Dowayos of Cameroon explained to me. 'We cry from joy and sing from grief.' At least, I think that is what they said. The word 'grief' was a little problem-atical to translate and then they both cried and sang – and even whistled a rather jolly tune – at funerals.

In fact, 'funeral' is a very broad category, rather like 'party'. A dinner party at the palace can be a fearful ordeal of rigid hierarchy, decodable into little else but statements of formal relationships of relative 'place'. The food will be inedible and largely irrelevant. An undergraduate party can be a wild festival of unstructure, senses jammed by drink, music and flashing lights, a sexual free-fire zone where anything goes and the loss of identity and hierar-

*After Fortune, 1932:186

chy is one of the avowed aims of the event. Both are parties. Funerals around the world can show the same huge range of variation from rigid formality to blind disorder. The word funeral is what has been termed an 'odd-job-word'.

The Yoruba of Nigeria say that they mourn a young person but celebrate the full life of an old one, so people may 'feel' differently at different sorts of funerals. Parents are not even allowed to attend the funerals of their dead children since it is the latter who should bury their parents, not vice versa, and it is expected that bereaved parents will be beyond all decent behaviour. Gravediggers will joke while digging the grave for an elder. For anyone younger, it is strictly forbidden.

It was noted by Rita Astuti* that at the memorial cross-raising ceremonies of the Vezo of Madagascar, those for children may be solemn and stress death, with only hymns. Those for the 'good dead', who have died after full lives, are cheerful, stress rebirth and have loud music.

Most cultures have an idea about the natural course of a life. It is deeply upsetting when young people die before old ones, or before attaining maturity. In Ghana, it is not unusual for the grandchildren of the deceased to turn up at the funeral, do a cheerful dance and announce that they will not mourn because it is only right that the old should die before the young.

Usually, the opposite is perceived as a disturbance of what is morally right. It will evoke accusations of witchcraft in an attempt to allocate blame on stigmatized groups. The phenomenon occurs among ourselves in response to AIDS.

*Astuti, 1994

Death is often marked by play on communication. The bereaved are cut off and separated from the rest of the world, bereft of faculties, socially mutilated. As a Nigerian explained mourning to me, 'You shave your head and take the phone off the hook.'

A common feature is explosions, the firing of guns, the beating of gongs – mere noise. We expect deep grief to reduce us to inarticulate sobs, make us incapable of speech; our formal mark of death is a minute's silence. So heavily is grief marked by silence that we find it impossible, immodest and embarrassing even to try to put the fact of death into words, the widow typically showing her appreciation of the mourner's sympathy by brave but tight-lipped hand-grasping through a soggy hankie. Among the Western Apache, the positions are reversed. The bereaved are held to be close to madness and should not be spoken to by normal people who may be harmed by their crazy talk.

Yet in the Shakespearean tradition, emotion leads to compulsive punning and verbal conceits, the flashing short-circuits of language showing the disarticulation of the universe. 'Put out the light, and then put out the light,' quips Othello, switching from thoughts of darkness to thoughts of death – unless pedantic emendors take a humourless quill to him. Around the world, grief is as likely to find expression in verbal artifice and poetic fireworks as mere noise or stillness of sound or motion. On the Polynesian island of Tikopia, wailing is called for but is heavily stylized and merges into poetic song and dance. Greatest eloquence may be evoked not by love songs, as in our own culture, but by death.

So the Alaskan Tlingit mourn largely, punningly and poignantly in song:

> Whenever I hear the sound of [the] thunder [bird]
> I become hurt.
> This sound reminds me of my lost uncle and brother.
> I am surprised when I hear thunder.
> It sounds like relatives I lost.*

*Kan, 1989:145

30

Such songs are performed at the funeral. Names are not mentioned, just kin categories, clan crests – like thunderbird – and are part of the ongoing wealth of the clan. Clan property, such songs may be used again and again and might refer to more than the immediate dead. Hence a group of mourners could sing the same song together with the same emotions but with quite different people in mind.

An alternative is alternation itself. In certain Australian groups, initially, loud lamentations may be appropriate. But at other parts of the ceremony, close relatives of the bereaved may be obliged to silence and immobility and some women may become silent and restricted to sign language for the rest of their lives. Amongst the Bwende of Central Africa, the obligation to cry may last so long that women have been known to go blind from constant weeping. Among the South American Jivaro, bereavement stresses blindness. The ghost of the dead stumbles around blindly knocking over pots and making noise, while the mourners have burning tobacco juice spat in their eyes and are forbidden sleep lest they see the dead.* And the dead may appear in forms that stress the dangers and limitations of sight – as staring owls or other beasts, or an almost invisible mist or as normal-looking creatures that are in fact hairy and repulsive and take away the living as pets. For it is above all the dead that feel desperate grief and loneliness and, like Dennis Nilsen, they kill for company.

For centuries, the Christian church sought to slip pious repentance as a final wafer in the mouth of the dying. But it had already undone itself by setting up the written will by which the rights of inheriting kin could be neatly side-stepped to enrich holy orders. The will gave the dying the certainty of the last word and the fight had been joined to allow the personal to show through the standard formulae that made death into a moral conclusion drawn from life. Like the recently popular American epitaph 'I Told You I Was Sick,' the urge to exit with a wisecrack rather than with

*Taylor, 1993

31

downcast eyes has often proved irresistible. The best walk a line between the obvious one-liner and the moral message. Who can top the wealth of malice betokened by Shakespeare's leaving to his wife his 'second-best' bed?

The eighteenth century was perhaps the high point of strained and self-conscious wit when a gentleman was required to depart this life with a sardonic smile on his lips. Edward Wortley Montagu, who died in 1776 aged 62, and distinguished by possessing an iron wig and a Turkish wardrobe, left a will as follows:

> ...I do not give his lordship any further part of my property because the best part of that he has contrived to take already. Item, to Sir Francis — I give one word of mine, because he has never had the good fortune to keep his own. Item, to Lord M— I give nothing because I know he'll bestow it on the poor. Item, to —, the author, for putting one in his travels, I give five shillings for his wit, undeterred by the charge of extravagance, since friends who have read his book consider five shillings too much. Item, to sir Robert W— I leave my political opinions, never doubting he can well *turn* them into cash, who has always found such an excellent market in which to *change* his own. Item, my cast-off habit of swearing oaths I give to Sir Leopold D—, in consideration that no oaths have ever been able to find him yet.

There had long been the earthier tradition of scaffold speeches of alternate brilliant insight and self-blindness. Monsieur Mayse, a Frenchman convicted of the killing of his son, limited himself to shouting at the executioner, 'What! Would you kill the father of a family?' There is a strange fascination in compilations of these famous last words. Their finality lends them a weight they cannot often bear. Goethe's 'mehr licht,' 'more light', interpreted as everything from a request to open the shutters to a demand for further advances in the Age of Enlightenment, is a case in point. One's greatest sympathy goes to Pancho-Villa, who summed up the whole genre: 'Don't let it end like this. Tell them I said something clever.'

Scaffold orations have recently staged a comeback in the

unlikely form of the American post-mortem video. Added to such terrors of life as the best-man's speech and the funeral oration there is now the requirement to make an autobiographical film that will be played to loved ones after one's death and even to descendants yet unborn. Stricken by mortality, we are no longer allowed to be passive but must speak our piece, make our statement. We must perform, prodded to the end by Western notions of the active subject. Some are so overcome by sudden celebrity that they virtually rise from deathbeds and tapdance their way through 'I Did It My Way'. Yet these performances have rapidly become standardized. Most are sickly-sweet and maundering, dwelling on love and support given, the eyes morphine-crazed, the smile rigid and fixed, the words as pointless and trite as the obligatory holiday postcard. Whatever is written on such cards, by the mere fact of their being sent, the message is 'Wish you were here.' That of the video reduces to much the same as the words of the grinning medieval skeletons of church murals. 'As you are now so once were we/And as we are so shall you be.'

There are occasional human touches. I watched one, of a frail old lady in a knitted pink bedcoat, who mouthed the usual orthodoxies celebrating the togetherness of family life and the values of contemporary America while alone in a solitary room in a hospital. At the end of it, perhaps under the impression that it would be edited, she looked at someone beyond the camera and said, 'Is that enough? Is that what they want? Ah, what the hell. You're all full of crap.'

—⚬⚬⚬—

For us smiles and laughter have no place at funerals. They are deeply shocking. A blanket of straight-faced formality covers all. I recall as a child watching a Remembrance Day parade in the village in which we lived. Troops marched past. Onlookers removed their hats and held them in their hands despite the rain. They were followed by line after line of old soldiers, medals pinned to fusty suit jackets, solemnly in step with bowler hats on their heads and umbrellas militarily sloped like rifles. As a pious child, it seemed to me an attempt at burlesque in the worst possible taste, a guying of military manners, for surely cheap wit had no place at a commemoration of the dead. I tried to point this out to bystanders and was shushed and finally slapped to teach me to 'show respect'.

To the Nyakyusa of Malawi the sobriety of an English burial is astonishing: 'We talk and dance to comfort the relatives. If we others sat sad and glum then the grief of the relatives would far exceed ours. If we just sorrowed what depths of grief would they not reach? And so we sit and talk and laugh and dance until the relatives laugh too.'*

Smiles and laughter have the same ambivalent relationship with internal states as tears and are not necessarily universal signs of joy. It is rightly said of Thais that they have a smile for every emotion. A colleague who worked in West Africa at the end of the Second World War could never explain why, when she showed local people the first pictures coming out of the concentration camps at that time, they laughed.

Yet comedy and indulgence too have their place at death. Madness and pantomime, the slapstick flinging of excrement and insults, attempts to copulate with one's grandmother or the deceased, heavy sexual trading, gluttony and drunkenness are all well documented as part of regular, obligatory funeral arrangements.

The Nyakyusa man who compared the impact of death to exasperating insults points to a common theme. The Nyakyusa have 'funeral friends' whose allotted task is to constantly insult and exasperate the dead and bereaved, who may not take offence. This is commonly the case in Africa and elsewhere with certain classes

*Wilson, 1939:24

34

of people, notably cross-cousins, relatives through marriage, 'blood brothers', age-mates, circumcision partners – those at the outer edges of kinship. They may make free with each others' property, molest each others' spouses, slander their mothers. They are traditionally called 'joking partners'. Yet theirs is also a serious job. We fondly imagine that in death 'primitive peoples' look after their own and we are indeed urged to follow their example. Very often this is not the case. Intimate contact with one's own dead may be deeply suspect since witches are characterized as having sex with or eating their own. Intermediaries are essential in dealing with the dead.

It is like the Northern English pig phenomenon explained to me as a child by my grandparents. Each family raised a pig, for slaughter, on household scraps. But you could not kill your own pig. That would be immoral. Instead, you swapped pigs with the neighbours and killed theirs, in that way holding death and grief at the right social distance. As the LoDagaa of Ghana put it, 'A person with a long face cannot suck his own wound.'

Jokers are the people who perform the most polluting acts, including those at a funeral. They wash and shave the body, sometimes massage the excrement from it, dispose of personal items, get down into the grave and manhandle the corpse. Among the LoDagaa, they bind the relatives of the dead to restrain their grief and do so in a way corresponding to the assessed strength of the kinship attachment to the dead. So a dead man's daughter is bound just by string about the foot. A dead woman's husband is tied with hide and cloth at the wrist and by string about waist and ankle.

Sometimes joking relationships extend to whole clans. Among the Gogo of Tanzania there may be a more or less historical relationship of previous enmity, now overcome in the mixed hostility and closeness of joking. There is endless ribbing about each others' clan names and tampering with relationship terms. Often death itself is a subject of jokes with a joking partner convincing his mate – April Fool-like – that a relative who is perfectly well has died so that he joyfully makes him grieve publicly for one yet alive.

Among the Ambo of Zimbabwe, the relations of the clans are expected to mirror those of life so that the Penis clan is superior to the Grass clan since water is shed by the former on the latter. Jokes centre on this.

The joking insults at funerals are, appropriately, double-edged, walking a line between aggression and solace. They use anomaly, dirt, insult and ambiguity to express the nature of a dangerous and marginal event – death itself. However, heavy reliance on 'anomaly' and 'marginality' in analyses of funeral rites is an excellent way for anthropologists to mask sections where the analysis just does not fit. It is curious that joking has never been seen as expressing a final spark of individuality in the deceased and the mourners. This would surely be the case in the interpretation of similar Western rites (such as the disposal of ashes) but then anthropologists have been keen to stress the 'communal' nature of non–Western life and death and find contrasts with ourselves. In the West no man is an island but many a man is depicted as a strangulated isthmus and every change in the rituals surrounding death over the past thousand years, from the introduction of gravestones to that of cremation, is seen as the forward march of individualism. In the writings of anthropologists on the sociality of African death, the triumph of the group over the individual is an endlessly reiterated theme that amounts to little more than an urging of the sick to 'lie back and think of Africa.'

Joking between the living, or the living and the dead? The Mexican Day of the Dead seems to be an example where there is a joking relationship with death itself. Once a year, around All Saints' Day (1 November), the dead are welcomed back to the land of the living and royally entertained. They will be offered new clothes, drinks and delicacies. Local usages vary with Church authorities urging 'respect' and sobriety, tradition preferring high jollity, excess and dancing. In places, men dress up as women to dance. The dead may be guided to the homes of their relatives by trails of marigolds or feasts and music may be brought to the graveyards. Skulls of sugar paste are exuberantly iced or made of chocolate for the children to suck. Papier mâché, sugar, tin and paper figures show the dead engaged in all the occupations of life. They use the phone, ride in trams, sell newspapers, or themselves, on street corners. So the dead hold up a mirror to the living and can be used for social or political satire, in the sort of magical realism literati are pleased to find as typical of South American literature.

A curious parallel exists in the form of certain nightlights currently on sale in London. They are double insulated, earthed, low-voltage, low-heat output – as obsessively safe as they can be made. But the bulb illuminates a bright orange, grinning Jack o'Lantern face with death's head attributes. Such a face, emblematic of trite horror but palpably phony and unreal, dispels any realistically imaginable terrors of the dark.

The Betsileo of Madagascar have attracted much missionary disapproval for their gusto in marking a funeral. While the body is still above ground, they have fights between men and bulls, drink to the point of unconsciousness and cover their faces with the cloths used as shrouds to engage in blind, orgiastic and incestuous sex. 'I am drunk! I am an animal!' they cry. Even sisters are not respected.

A story tells that among the first Betsileo, couples had already had children. 'One of these children died. There was weeping and lamentation and people complained to God. God sent his son to find out what had happened. The boy came to earth and felt great pity for the poor people. He returned to heaven and asked permission from his father to resuscitate the dead child. Then, he returned to earth. But these journeys had taken a long time, and on his arrival on earth he found the people dancing and singing, already having forgotten their dead. He became indignant and once more returned to his father. "They're not sad any more and are having fun," he told him. "What's the point of bringing the dead back to life?" Since this time, men die.'*

Roughhouse and ribaldry were not always foreign to English

*Dubois, 1938:1334

funerals. Medieval clerics constantly inveighed against the traditional practices at the wakes that were finally driven underground by the Puritan dictatorship. The seventeenth-century antiquarian Aubrey recorded the following description of a Yorkshire funeral:

> They continue the custom of watching and sitting up all night till the body is interred. In the interim some kneel down and pray, some play at cards, some drink and take tobacco: they have also mimical plays and sports e.g. they choose a simple young fellow to be a judge, then the suppliants (having first blacked their hands by rubbing it under the bottom of the pot), beseech his Lordship and smut all his face. They play likewise at hot cockles.*

This was apparently a game involving one person being blindfolded while others struck at his private parts.

Denunciation of funeral games forms part of the endless liturgical controversy of the sixteenth century. Yet we should beware of seeing regulations forbidding certain practices as firm proof they were, in fact, going on. After all, while it is still prohibited to transport lighted gas lamps and funerary masonry on the London Underground system this plays no major role in our own normal funerary procedure.

Most British rituals involve a 'joke' slot, a section where the individual is allowed free expression and eccentricity is cultivated. In the British wedding ceremony it is how the bride arrives at the church. They come on horseback, bicycle and milkman's float. They hang-glide into the graveyard or descend from balloons. Absurdity is all.

The usual joke slot in the British funeral is the disposal of the ashes. The British body itself is held to be subject to all manner of controls and 'respect', though the law is much laxer than popularly assumed. There is little to stop a properly certified body being

*Aubrey, 1881:30

buried anywhere though Hindu river disposals can fall foul of water regulations. Ashes, however, known in the trade as 'cremains', are no longer a body. Cremation seems for many nowadays to be a clean and accelerated way of avoiding the horrors of physical decay. The body has been reduced to a formless and inoffensive grey powder, finally put through an electric grinder to avoid the possibility of any lingering recognition. It is these ashes that are the subject of riotous and competitive eccentricity.

What can one do with ashes? The whole business of cremation and scattering seems obviously to imply a dissolution of identity but the fixing of manner and place reinjects the individual back into the operation. A scientist from Macclesfield recently made the awkward stipulation that his ashes be scattered from a rocket of his own devising, but a similar dispersal was achieved earlier this century by Sir Clough Williams Ellis who used special fireworks for the purpose. A comforting, eco-friendly circularity can be derived from cremains used as fertilizer on some favoured plant or lawn, an unnatural process masquerading as natural. They can also become a weapon of offence. A museum colleague has decreed that his ashes shall be flung in the eyes of the Trustees of the British Museum. A certain pettish art critic has designated his to be mixed with breadcrumbs and scattered on the steps of the National Gallery, there to be reprocessed by pigeons as 'action painting' that will communicate his views on such art to the Gallery's trustees. A pub landlord has had himself converted into the contents of an egg-timer 'so that he can carry on working'. Most, however, want their ashes to be where their heart was, thereby seeking something greater than their own compromised individuality. Nowadays football clubs receive so many requests for ashes to be scattered on their pitches that outbreaks of goalmouth baldness have occurred and official guidelines have had to be issued: 'There is no need to scatter all the ashes. You can scatter a sample . . . On a windy day it is best to scatter ashes upwind . . .'

Manchester United, it seems, receives some 20–25 requests a year, Bolton Wanderers a mere four. Lord's cricket ground, perhaps understandably, refuses to have any truck whatever with ashes.

Anthropologists like to interpret boisterousness of language and sexual behaviour at funerals as marking a 'return to life', a confrontation of death with a vigorous statement of fleshly pleasures or a moderation of grief through joking. There are other explanations. The Shona of Zimbabwe, like the ancient Greeks, stress the revivifying effect of chaos itself as a return to a primeval state. 'The very source of life is portrayed as primordial union – a lack of distinction between heaven and earth, high and low, man and woman, me and you.'*

The Dobuans of Melanesia stress replacement rather than chaos, the fact that one person steps into the shoes of another and takes his name, and they even rejuggle kinship terms to fit with the new assumed identity. Some societies, like the LoDagaa, seem reluctant to waste any of the social relationships in which a person may be involved. The end of a funeral involves vigorous miming of the activities of all the groups in which the deceased was engaged and a redistribution of social roles. Even the position of friend and lover may be inherited by others and rewoven into the altered network of relations.

At an individual level, seemingly cathartic 'jokers' may not cause hilarity in the objects of their attentions and are directly motivated by the wish to extract payment to stop such intensely annoying behaviour. Ritual joking may not involve 'real' amusement any more than ritual mourning involves 'real' grief. If it has a healing effect at all it is perhaps less because jokers are a source of innocent merriment than that they are a counter-irritant.

I was in my late twenties and had just seen my first dead body, an African, Dowayo, body. The segregation of the living and the dead is so complete in Britain that I had never actually *seen* any of the various relatives who had died during my childhood. Usually I had not even gone to the funeral. It was not something for a child, hushed up like an obscenity, one of those subjects that made adults drop into whispers. Like most formative experiences, my first

*Jacobson-Widding and van Beek, 1990:40

40

dead body had actually been curiously ordinary and matter-of-fact. People gathered round the corpse, smoking, making jokes about its skinny legs. They briskly trussed it up in a business-like way in the pose adopted by boys when they are circumcized, tumbled it deftly into a cattle skin, tucking and stitching, with all the practised gestures of professional gift-wrappers.

Inevitably I was writing notes and a crowd had gathered to watch me watching them, more interested in that than the relative commonplace of death. 'What happens to a man's powers/soul/spirit after he dies?' I tried querulously, like a vicar hoping to get a current affairs discussion going at a youth club. They ignored me. Then one man turned round and snapped, 'How should I know? Am I God?'

There was a great deal of watching going on. A joking partner of the dead man was staring at me and 'writing notes' in the dust with his backside shoved high in the air. He grabbed his chin and strode arrogantly about nodding his head before returning to his doodling in the sand. The bystanders liked that and laughed and clapped. 'See. He is just like the white man.' There were no women there because the men circumcized at the same time as the deceased had just exposed themselves to the body, plucking off penis sheaths and waving their organs of enthusiasm in the faces of the onlookers. A woman, it was known, would die if she saw such a thing and they had all fled inside the huts when they realized what was about to happen. 'It's only thanks to me you were circumcized!' the men screamed at the corpse, the greatest insult you can offer a fellow male.

Earlier they had tried to steal the dead body and ransom it but there had been some sort of an altercation with the special clown hired for the festival, not a joking partner, but privileged to take liberties and handle the body for the duration of the event. The exact nature of the event, it had to be admitted, was a little confused. This man had just died but offstage they were wrapping the skulls of men who had died years ago so that two different stages of a funeral had got entangled. Who were these clowns, anyway? Was it two different sorts of people intersecting in the same ritual space? Had they really fought? Where two clowns were concerned it was hard to tell where simple 'reality' lay and the joke began. At the last funeral, they had killed a mouse, flayed it and danced with the skin in mockery of the cow killed to wrap the corpse.

The chief was beside me looking furtive. He had taken part in the earlier jollities but was now uneasy. Two of his *duuse*, a class of joking relative descended from a common great-grandfather, were also *duuse* of the deceased and they were rampaging about somewhere in the village, old men, both very drunk. If they found him in all his funeral finery they would take his hat and sunglasses, humiliate him in public and there was nothing he could do about it. They were working hard at becoming my *duuse* too, arguing that, since the chief had adopted me, they had the right to pillage my stores, smash my equipment and shout obscenities in my face. It was, I would be told, part of being accepted by the local people. Having the right to tell lies as well, they seemed like a picture of fieldwork assistants from Hell. 'Cunt, cunt, cunt. The cunt of the beer!' they uttered in a screaming falsetto. It blew across the cheerful chatter of the crowd.

There they were, one row of huts away, staggering against the thatch, beer dregs around their mouths, shorts askew, pushing and shoving like giggling schoolboys. The chief and I shot each other a look of pain and fatigue and scuttled off to hide. The crowd liked that too. They clapped and cheered again, pointing out delightedly to the old men which way we had run.

In ethnographic accounts, it is clear that joking relationships occur quite widely in social life – at birth, illness, problems with the fields – but joking at funerals has been picked out and emphasized largely because it confronts Western views of 'natural' behaviour. It presents itself as something to be explained. There is also a more general pattern whereby 'respect' relationships are held to be the opposite of those of joking. The reason that joking relationships in death have so obsessed Westerners is that funerals demand from us a response that is every bit as artificial and 'ritual' but opposed. Instead of joking, we take up exaggerated postures of respect.

So when the Tetum of Timor celebrate birth by standing either side of a new-born child, piling ridiculous and hilarious insults on each other and end up having water fights we see no problem. It is, after all, a happy occasion. That peoples do similar things at funerals is puzzling because it seems to show lack of respect.

The word recurs endlessly in our reaction to death. We attend funerals 'to pay our respects', remove our hats in the presence of the dead 'to show respect', dress in black to be 'respectful'. In the past, anthropologists have even tried to build the notion into their general analyses by setting off a category of solemn 'ceremonial' from mere 'ritual'.

'Never speak ill of the dead,' we are told and indeed our culture offers a paramount example of one where the dead, in the short term at least, must be converted into idealized memories. Only later may they be reassessed and 'rubbished'. So, on his death, President Nixon went overnight from 'living crook' to 'dead elder statesman'.

The language about the dead, like that of Wimbledon tennis commentaries, is one of polite euphemism and understatement. A recent spat between a Lancashire vicar and his flock, carried to the highest Church authority, centred on whether the gravestone should contain the word 'father' or 'dad'. The family wanted the latter, since that is what they had called the deceased. The vicar insisted on the former as a gravestone is a public funeral document. 'It will not be long before we have Cuddles, Squidgy and Ginger, which would make the last resting place sound like a pets' cemetery.' The family lost, but maybe got off lightly. They might have had 'the dear departed'.

The obituary writer must be a master of the unexpressed criticism. The ill-tempered and opinionated dead 'do not suffer fools gladly'. The narrow-minded are 'focused' and 'dedicated'. Sluts 'give generously of themselves' and dirty old men become 'gay old dogs.' The dead are recreated in a language of exclusively positive

43

sugar-frosted nuances so as to be 'made over', sometimes becoming virtually unrecognizable.

The difference between the language of obituaries and other prose was inadvertently demonstrated by a German colleague of mine when her normally impeccable English deserted her at the funeral of a friend. She referred to his obituaries as 'reviews'.

It is not surprising that death itself should be avoided in speech around the world. Death quite literally disrupts the flow of language, both at the individual and the social level, and is at best a bearable disorder in the flow of life. It lends itself to euphemistic recasting. In the language of political correctness you 'fail to fulfil your wellness potential' or 'suffer terminal inconvenience'. The idiom of absence is invoked by the Laymi of Bolivia who say that a dead person has 'gone to cultivate chilli pepper'. Among the Alaskan Tlingit you have 'gone up into the woods'. A Malay dictionary offers an insight into cultural classifications with *mampus* meaning 'to die (of beasts and pagans), never used of Muslims'. Other languages may have words for particular kinds of death yet no general word for death in all its aspects.

Sporting idioms provide 'take an early bath' or 'peg out' (from croquet or cribbage) or 'hear the final whistle'. Theology 'gives up the ghost' or 'goes to meet his maker'. Old euphemisms gain new motivations. When someone now 'expires', he is no longer seen as giving up the divine breath of life. Rather, his death is relegated to a bureaucratic world of overdue library books and invalid season tickets.

Yet, there is also an inverse tendency within the language of death, a deliberate stressing of the concrete and physical in a rich brew of metonymic slang, just as the body itself may be subject to insult as well as respect. So, in Mexico you 'stretch out your legs' or, nowadays, 'chuck your trainers', an equivalent of the Northern English 'pop your clogs'. In German you 'get cold feet', in French 'eat dandelions by the roots' and in English 'push up the daisies' or 'bite the dust'.

The human body is not a singular thing. It is at the intersection of several vocabularies so that we have the erotic, medical and popular bodies all carved up differently in language. The proliferation of terms plucked from all these and incongruously mixed to replace the alleged factuality of medical death reflects that the body, semantically if not always ritually, is at the crossroads.

2

Before and after the Fact

'No problem is insoluble given a big enough plastic bag'
Tom Stoppard

On market days, it was always a good idea to sit on the tree trunk outside the village. There was an unbroken stream of people coming down from the hills and heading into town, bearing leaves, yams and small livestock. Later, the flow would be reversed and they would pass by again carrying cloth, sugar and beer up into the granite heights. But whether they had traded or not, their tread would be a little less steady, indeed most would be drunk, and there would be plenty of new gossip. By sitting there for a few hours, you could find out everything that had happened in the known world.

A figure appeared in the distance, wheeling a green bicycle with a huge bundle of leaves strapped to the back, a green cloche hat slapped on his head, a long green raincoat irregularly buttoned and too short in the arms, revealing bare legs and wrists like a flasher: Pascal. He parked the bike carefully, sat down, and smiled, running splayed fingers over his face in a very African gesture of fatigue. He then wiped them on his thigh and offered his hand in a courtly handshake.

'Where's *Taab gaay*?'

Pascal was a bit of a city slicker so we spoke French. It was an old joke but he giggled. *Taab gaay* – where is the tobacco? – the invariable first words of his wife on seeing me. By a long-standing unspoken agreement, we pretended I thought it was her name.

'She died last night.'

I was shocked. He seemed very nonchalant about it. I dithered, and at the last minute resisted asking what she had died of. In the Dowayo world, this was always too complicated for simple enquiry. She might have been killed by ancestors or witchcraft or the power of her own sorcery, or by a Western disease, or by any combination of these. The truth would emerge only gradually.

'What happened?'

'She was just walking about, felt dizzy and died.'

I stammered out consolation and as I did so Pascal looked over my head, waved and grinned. Looking up, I saw his wife walking slowly down the road, pulling idly at leaves on either side, dressed in cloth and heading for town. I felt a flash of anger that he had played such a silly trick. Then I remembered. Amongst the Dowayos, anyone who faints or goes into a coma is described as 'dead'; death is a much less cut-and-dried affair than amongst ourselves. Stories abound of people who have revived after the wrapping of their bodies has already begun. It is not that such people are not truly dead, or that some sort of metaphor is being used to say that fainting is 'like death'. Indeed, people insist, they *are* dead. But then they simply stop being dead. Death is not a point, it is a continuing process, and sometimes the process may go into reverse and the dead may revive.

Already *Taab gaay* was wetting her lips and smiling, looking at the cigarettes in my top pocket. I knew what her first question would be.

It might seem obvious that the universality of death lies less in the emotions it calls forth than in the state of death itself. After all, you're either dead or not and there can't be much doubt about it. In the West, we have made our inability to conquer death into a virtue. Death is the Ultimate Universal Fact from which there is no escape, its harsh reality resisting any theory or doctrine that would shape or domesticate it. There is no way round death, no negotiation possible. We even realize that our own attempts to deny it are ultimately futile. So, corresponding to its negative power is a positive sense in which its brutal factuality takes on moral value. It is the crowning glory of our culture's pragmatic materialism, comforting proof of the factuality of what is actually a socially constructed world. The universality of death is the proof of the universality of our world.

Yet the biological facts of death have little relation to our culturally orthodox views. At the social level, male is normally the 'unmarked' sex and death is held to be an abnormal intrusion into life. But at the cellular level, female is the 'unmarked' sex and cell death, apoptosis, is built into our genetic programming. Constant messages, interruptions in the smooth running of the programme, are required to prevent our body components committing mass suicide. The only cells that are truly immortal – paradox again – are the cancerous cells that kill us in increasing numbers.

'Immortalization', if not immortality, is a fact. It refers to the process by which human cells can be infected with viral DNA to generate a human cell-line that can be endlessly produced outside the body for research purposes. Such cells can be used to test drugs on a standard gene-stock or produce useful compounds for the treatment of disease in ways that would not be possible on living individuals. So one prominent drug company produces Interferon from the Namalwa cell line, derived from the body of an African girl of that name who died of lymphatic cancer.

Recently, a Californian, John Moore, sued to regain control over products derived from the immortalized cells of his own surgically-removed spleen. The case hinged on whether such cells remained essentially part of his own body or whether they were merely raw material, analogous to grapes used in the manufacture of wine. The court ruled that you have no property rights over parts of your body that have been removed in the course of surgery.

At a higher cellular level, eternity belongs only to cancer cells. Henrietta Lacks of Baltimore died over forty years ago but her cell-line lives on around the world in research laboratories as HeLa and its children. Like the fragments of the true cross, the authenticated remains now far exceed the mass of her original body.

———

Phlogiston and the human soul are, for me, inextricably interlinked. Scientists and theologians are expected to be dotty and at school they were encapsulated for me in a single person – Bert. Bert was possessed of deep faith in both science and religion as signified by his madman's haircut, his loud singing of hymns and his alternation of films about the nitrogen cycle with unctuous American evangelical offerings. Both were randomly projected in a room full of Bunsen burners, retort flasks and other tokens of scientific rationality. The doubtful idea was that both invoked the same standards of dispassionate evidence. Bert particularly liked one image of a huge cardboard drum of chemicals mixed into a grey, vaguely crystalline powder. 'Every chemical constituent of a human body,' the presenter smirked, running it through his fingers. 'But it's *not* a living human. What's missing? The divine spirit.'

Even at that stage of unawareness, I noted its echoes in Bert's talks combining rabbit reproduction and moral uplift. 'Sex before marriage,' he offered, 'is like a pair of football boots. All very well in themselves. But what's missing? The spirit of the game.'

The phlogiston theory of combustion was something so close to Bert's heart that it's a wonder he ever got beyond it. It's a way into many Western assumptions about the nature of the world – the idea that force involves matter, that essences are 'real'. In the eighteenth century, when things burnt, it seemed reasonable to suppose that something was present and used up on each occasion, a fire principal, phlogiston. Bert taught us that the theory was refuted in a classic series of experiments by Lavoisier, in the eighteenth century, on the grounds that as things burned they *gained* rather than lost weight.

In fact, I now discover, this was not true, Bert did us false. It was suggested at the time, quite reasonably, that phlogiston might have negative weight – an idea far less counter-intuitive than many of modern particle physics. Phlogiston became easily confused with lighter-than-air substances such as hydrogen whose existence could be empirically demonstrated. The question of the testability of the phlogiston hypothesis, then, depends less on evidence than the decision at what point final authority is to be accorded to 'common sense' notions rather than 'scientific' ones.

The anthropologist E. B. Tylor speculated that the belief in death as the loss of the soul was cobbled together from objective observation of the dead body and the subjective experience of dreaming. The soul would be, in such a view, a hypothesis that was a sort of spiritual phlogiston. Why not repeat Lavoisier's experiments in search of the soul?

There is a recent report of a Düsseldorf doctor who placed the beds of his patients on a set of extremely sensitive scales. At the moment of death, in repeated experiments, he noted a loss of weight of twenty-one grammes. The weight of a human soul? Daedalus (Dr David Jones) of the scientific periodical *Nature* has provocatively suggested that by attaching piezolelectric transducers, inertial-navigation accelerometers and other instruments to the dying, it would also be possible to measure the direction, velocity and 'spin' of a soul as it leaves the body and makes it recoil slightly. A soul should be easier to track than a quark.

Meanwhile, Dr Peter Fenwick of the Institute of Psychiatry has arranged for messages to be placed near the ceiling in a coronary intensive care unit. The idea is that this is a frequent place for out-of-body, near-death experiences. Such people typically see themselves or their souls as rising into the air and looking down on their own bodies from a dissociated state. If they are really up there, they should be able to read what is written near the ceiling and accurately report it on their recovery. Bert would have understood all these efforts.

Other cultures often see the body as an open-ended receptacle of forces much more complex than that covered by the simple Western division into body and soul. A person exists where an identity and a body temporarily coincide but components may be added or lost, or may grow or diminish. Our creation of terms such as 'social identity' simply seeks to generalize a Western division of the world into material and non-material and while useful for brutal comparisons often does violence to the thought of others.

The awkwardness of the European soul comes largely from the fact that Christianity is a religion designed by committee. Until a major revision in AD 869 asserting that Man was made exclusively of Body and Soul, there was a third term, the Psyche, that moved easily between the two. The Samo of Upper Volta number at least a dozen components of a human being that are difficult to include in either category. The Fang of Gabon have seven souls, the Dogon of Mali eight, of both sexes, and even share souls with their joking partners, the neighbouring Bozo.

The Avatip also have a view of the human constitution that resists simple classification.* They see a man's 'spirit' as starting out as more or less neutral animating energy. Through ritual transformation, it becomes ever more autonomous, concrete and dangerous until, amongst seniors, it takes up separate residence in a special net bag kept in the house on all but ritual occasions, something he can shrug on at appropriate times but keep safe at others.

In Haiti, the basic components are: the *corps cadavre*, the *n'ame*, the *étoile*, the *gros bon ange*, the *ti bon ange*. The first is the physical body.† The *n'ame* is the power that allows the individual cells of the body to function. The *gros bon ange* is undifferentiated energy that enters the body at conception and functions to keep it alive. The *étoile* is the individual's star of destiny and is in the sky. The *ti bon ange* is the personal aspect that involves character and willpower and leaves an individual while sleeping. Witchcraft

*Harrison, 1993:110
†Davis, 1988:186

51

involves stealing this power and it is the hijacking of this element that turns a person into a zombie, the living dead.

There is a beast in all of us. Almost all our DNA is shared with quite lowly forms of life. Humanity is a mere late addition in the margins of the blueprint. This view expresses itself variously in fields as diverse as ethology (the notion that Man is an ape with knobs on), psychiatry (the notion that wild urges within us are fighting to get out of the civilized shell) and strategic studies (the notion that war and aggression are endemic to the human condition). All these may be seen as a variant of totemism, the idea shared by many peoples that relations among animals are a good way of thinking about the human condition. Even a sort of medical totemism of laboratory animals has developed, according to medical resemblances between basic bodily systems. Pigs are best for experiments on circulation, monkeys for lungs, armadillos – intriguingly – for skin afflictions such as leprosy.

The Chamula Indians of Mexico hold that everyone has three souls. One is on the tip of the tongue and relates to the candle in the sky that predetermines his lifespan. The two others are animal soul-companions, living in corrals in the sky and the mountains.* The rich and powerful have jaguars and coyotes for companions. Lesser people have oppossum and squirrel companions. The animals fight and the weak may be savaged by the strong who may be companions of witches. Alternatively, the animals may escape from the corral or be sold to the earth god, or shot in ignorance by hunters. All these make the human companion ill and may even kill him. Hence death does not cause the loss of the soul. It is the loss of the soul that causes death.

Death is like every other category. It works well in a rough-and-ready way but attempts to define it lead to a sort of internal collapse. This typically happens where categories are forced ever further in a competitive situation. The setting of a water-speed record now involves a definition of the common-sense notion 'in

*Gossen, 1974:15

contact with the water'. The legal concept 'cause' in cases of
'causing the death' of someone requires that the effect, to be
accounted so, must occur within a year and a day of the alleged
cause. Now that comatose victims can be maintained alive for
years before succumbing, it has become impossible to charge their
murderers with causing their deaths. All such lines are ultimately
arbitrary. The symptoms of death – lack of respiration or heart-
beat, coldness and rigor mortis, opening of the sphincters, insen-
sitivity to electrical stimuli – may each occur without death. The
only sure and certain sign of death is the onset of putrefaction of
the corpse.

In their need to make organs available for transplant, doctors
have been obliged to try to pin down death leading to the spawn-
ing of subtypes – brain death, heart death. Kidney transplants
work best if the organs are removed from the donor while still a
'heart-beating cadaver', artificially maintained on a ventilator. In
attempts to control abortion, legislators have had to avoid equat-
ing the beginning of life with either conception or actual birth
and babies have been born from mothers who 'died' days before
but whose vital functions were maintained in order for the foetus
to continue to gestate. So we no longer even know where life and
death begin; their boundaries are periodically redefined like those
of warring states. Some hospitals in America now have philosophical consultants to advise on the issues raised by difficult decisions
concerning the boundary between life and death.

No Western death is considered real without a certificate that
explains the 'cause of death'. In the final days of capital punishment in Britain, the prisoner was hanged in the actual presence of
a doctor and then an inquest was immediately held to 'establish
the cause' of death and produce a certificate in due form that the
doctor would sign.

If you 'die' from cardiac arrest and are revived, despite now
being qualified to go into the Near-Death-Experience-Industry,
no certificate is issued, officially it never happened. If a child is
stillborn, the event is entered in a special register since it cannot be
officially either a birth or a death. It usually proves impossible to

secure Church burial for such a body since it has never been ecclesiastically 'born' let alone baptized.

Michael Kearl reports that in America in 1985, a major controversy erupted over the disposal of 16,433 aborted foetuses found in a steel bin.* The US Supreme Court was required to decide whether or not the foetuses should be turned over to a religious organization for disposal. The outcome was a fine sacred/secular compromise. The foetuses were given a non-religious burial as inert matter but with a eulogy written by President Reagan as if for people.

—◦◦◦—

'Do you know what that is?' my host reached out and patted a large bundle in one corner of his living room. It looked like the bundle of old clothes you pick out for the charity shop and then forget to take there for months. A child was circling it on a tricyle, mouthfarting motorbike noises. 'It's my grandmother.'

Before the advent of television, no Western house was complete without a granny to sit with the children and spout idiotic wisdoms at them. Many Torajan houses still have one, but she may be dead. The body is wrapped in vast amounts of absorbent cloth to soak up the juices of putrefaction. Quite quickly, the whole bundle becomes relatively inoffensive. Some modern Torajans cheat and use formalin to slow down decay while the family mobilize resources and collect absent members to move on to the next stage of the funeral. Food and drink will daily be put on a plate and balanced on the body.

'Aren't you going to greet her?'

'Pleased to meet you granny.' A gesture was difficult: a handshake was impossible, but it would have been overly familar to pat the bundle.

*Kearl, 1989:323

'Wah, that's good.'

'How long has she been dead?'

He looked at me appalled. 'We don't say that. She's 'sleeping' or 'has a headache'. She won't die until she leaves the house. She's been sleeping for three years now.'

He reached over and took down a huge cassette player to offer musical entertainment. The tapes, I noticed, were stored in alphabetical order on the body which made a handy shelf.

'You'll miss her when she dies,' I said.

It is striking how little other people's views on the borders of death coincide with our own. It has been suggested that among Australian Aborigines many deaths from cursing or witchcraft result from relatives withdrawing vital support from someone who is accounted 'as good as dead'. Victims, in the materialist Western view, die of simple dehydration.

In Joseph Heller's novel, *Catch-22*, there is a fanciful account of the sufferings of a man who is very much alive while officially dead. Among the Dogon of Mali, once the funerary rituals of an absent person, presumed dead, have been performed, he can no longer be accepted as living even if he returns. His family will refuse to recognize him and he will be reduced to destitution.

Recently, French newspapers have been much concerned with the story of Georges Verron, a seventy-four-year-old who, although alive, is officially dead. At the end of the war, his identity was hijacked by a collaborator who urgently needed new papers. When the imposter died, the government cut off Monsieur Verron's pension. Unable to convince the government of his identity, he cannot obtain a passport, bank account or make a will. He tried to sue the authorities but was told that this was impossible. A dead man cannot bring a lawsuit.

The opposite fate befalls Chinese who die abroad. On being brought home for burial they will be treated as alive and determinedly welcomed as such. They will officially 'die' only much later. Similarly, it has been pointed out that according to Hindu ritual, the deceased only 'dies' at the moment that the skull is split open on the funeral fire.* Technically, then, Hindu cremation is a *live* sacrifice. Conversely, an ascetic, who has long ago renounced the world through symbolic death, needs no further funeral rites at his demise and is slid directly into the Ganges without formality.

The anticipation of death finds its clearest application in the entombment of the living. In many cultures, it has been common to bury alive wives, servants, anyone particularly closely linked with the deceased. Between the twelfth and fifteenth centuries in the theocratic states of Europe, living saints were created by walling up recluses, especially women. They were normally entombed in marginal locations – bridges, city gates, the entries to cemeteries – only a small aperture being left for the provision of food or as a window giving a view of the church. Living symbols of the renunciation of the world of the flesh, their physical sufferings were catalogued in morbid detail and became accumulations of virtue and sources of divine capital. When the cults of purgatory in which suffering bought salvation declined, reclusion completely disappeared.

They emerged again in a much milder, consciously archaic and rustic form as the 'ornamental hermits' engaged by eighteenth-century aristocrats to agreeably animate the grounds of their country houses.

I well remember an early experience in the island of Eddystone in the Solomons when a man whom I knew well was seriously ill. I heard that he had been visited by a great native physician, who was shortly expected to return, and presently there came along the narrow bush-path the usual procession in single file, headed by the doctor who, in

*Parry, 1982

56

answer to my enquiries concerning his patient, mournfully shook his head and uttered the words '*Mate, mate.*' I naturally supposed that the end had come only to learn that all that was meant was that the man was still very seriously ill. As a matter of fact he recovered. The oldest man in the island, again was almost certainly over ninety years of age, and he was not only regarded as *mate*, though really one of the most alive people on the island, but in speaking of him people made use of an expression *manatu* which otherwise is only used in the religious formulae of the cult of the dead.

It is clear that it is wholly wrong to translate *mate* as dead or to regard its opposite *toa* as the equivalent of living. These people have no categories exactly corresponding to our 'dead' and 'living' but have two different categories of *mate* and *toa*, one including with the dead the very sick and the very aged, while the other excludes from the living those who are called *mate*... Even today the Melanesian does not wait until a sick man is dead in our sense, but if he is considered sufficiently *mate*, movements or even groans will furnish no ground for abandoning the funeral rites, or the process of burial, while a person who, through external interference is rescued from this predicament, may have a very unpleasant time, since it would seem that nothing would make such a man other than *mate* for the rest of his life.*

The Solomons situation is not that different from contemporary Britain. In theory, death is a moment, a time, that can be recorded on a certificate; yet there have always been beliefs about residual death. In the nineteenth century it was still believed that the wounds of a murder victim would shed blood in the presence of the killer. In the twentieth century, French doctors seriously researched allegations that the severed heads of the guillotined followed you around the room with their eyes like the Mona Lisa. Despite the neat, slicing divisions of language and documentation, social identity runs like a smooth parabola and one's place along it is measured by command over one's own body. Children only gradually assume responsibility for, and authority over their excretory, digestive and sexual functions. Growing up consists of

*W. H. Rivers, *Psychology and Ethnology*, 1926: 41

numerous domestic battles over control of hair, clothes, food, drink, sexual orifices by which boundaries of proprietorship are pushed forward until entry into complete social adulthood is marked by full ownership of one's own form. Before this time, even with consent, tattooing constitutes assault as does sexual intercourse.

Special states involve a loss of adult rights over one's body. Serious disease results in assigning powers to others and a temporary regression to infantile states of compliance in feeding, excretion etc. at a hospital. Criminality is punished by reduced adulthood similarly marked. Old age is expected to bring gradual erosion of bodily ownership and control until death brings a complete surrender of social identity and the total loss of the body again. The dead do not own their own corpses.

Who you are informs where you lie on this parabola. Sociologists have suggested that the point at which one is likely to be defined as 'dying' in a Western hospital, with all the potentially lethal withdrawal of care that that involves, depends as much on class and social status as on medical history.

Other cultures home in on language to define where you are in life. A child has no language. Social maturity is marked by oral skill. The Chamba of the Cameroon/Nigerian border hold that the incomprehensible babbling of infants and the old is the language of the spirit world. The former have not yet forgotten it, the latter are resuming it, hence their affinity with each other. The Baule of Ivory Coast maintain that it is dangerous even to bring together two babies still babbling ancestral language. They might plot against the living. The Alaskan Tlingit were convinced of the danger of yawning. To the living it is silent. But in the language of the dead it is a loud sound.

—◦◦◦—

Zombies, it seems, are real. They actually exist. Death is not a one-way ticket. An ethnobiologist, Wade Davis, has met some.* We have a photograph of a zombie sitting, appropriately, on his own grave with his arms crossed in apparent resignation. James Bond and a hundred other 'tuppenny dreadfuls' have planted a wilder iconography firmly in our minds – grinning skulls, obscene midnight rites, the glassy-eyed stomping tread of the homicidal corpse, arms spread for crushing and strangling. Papa Doc Duvalier cultivated his own resemblance to Baron Samedi, head of the Voodoo pantheon, by affecting the dress of a conservative undertaker while hooking his administration into the traditional network of secret societies that ruled urban Haiti from the slave revolts of the eighteenth century on. The conflict between the Tonton Macoute and Bertrand Aristide is a rerun of ancient clashes between urban voodoo and creole Catholicism. Yet in Davis's account, the Bizango secret society, the major cult of voodoo, ends up sounding rather like a branch of the Rotary Club with its emphasis on group and traditional family values. Actual zombification is rarely achieved and involves the administration of orthodotoxin – the poison in Japanese puffer-fish – to simulate death in the victim. After his burial, zombie masters drag the conscious but paralysed zombie from his grave and lead him off to a drug-dependent career as a slave in a country awash with cheap labour. A very few such cases are enough to convince the population of the power of the association and lead their feet into the paths of virtue.

West African roots are prominent. Yet the striking thing about Haitian zombifications is how unlike African zombie beliefs they are. In a classic study of the Bakweri of West Cameroon, Edwin Ardener has shown that accusations of zombie masterhood come in sporadic waves.[†] It is the people who enjoy conspicuous success at the expense of their relatives who are held to be zombie owners. They prey on their own kin, killing them with witchcraft,

*Davis, 1988
†Ardener, 1970

and shipping them off to work in zombie mines and factories in the mountains. Their wages fall to their betrayers' lot.

Both sets of beliefs about death are a base for what may be termed 'anti-yuppie cults'. The Haitian reduces the self-seeking to slavery in a society whose historical charter of freedom is a slave rebellion. The Cameroonian exposes him to potentially fatal witchcraft accusation in a country where it is not unknown for leaders to sell out their followers. In both cases, the possession of a tin roof is a notorious giveaway of excessive individual wealth and in both places people are afraid to spend their personal income on one. The sin of wages can be death.

The fates of men after death can be quantified to produce a map of human wickedness. In 1993, the *Birmingham News* of Birmingham, Alabama, published a map of the damned, according to which 46.1 per cent of the people are headed for Hell. The map was produced by the Southern Baptist Convention to help its pastors search out concentrations of the greatest sinners. The unsaved were calculated by subtracting from each county's population the number of registered church members and applying a secret formula that predicts how many of each sect will go to Heaven. The formula allows a greater or lesser proportion to attain salvation according to their relative closeness to Baptist doctrine. More Methodists will be saved than Catholics. Jews, Buddhists and Hindus will all be damned.

3

The Mythical Place of Death

Small boy: 'Where do animals go when they die?'
Small girl: 'All good animals go to Heaven, but the bad ones go to
the Natural History Museum.'

E.H. Shepard, 1929

It was one of those interminable wet afternoons in an African village that are like a regression to childhood notions of time. It would feel like days till the evening came. Tomorrow morning, with its promise of market day, was several weeks away.

The day had been a bit of a failure. The rain chief had promised to come but had not turned up, delayed no doubt by the unforeseen storm. Tomorrow he would arrive and tell me all about how he had had to stay up his mountain and nobly turn away destructive winds from the valley. All I had for company were the schoolteacher and a couple of hunters caught in the rain, happy to sit and smoke my cigarettes and drink my coffee and look out of the door blankly at the water. Following a big local funeral, I had hoped to collect a lively myth about the origin of death, the sort of thing Africa specializes in. When I asked, they looked at me as if I were mad. 'Death? How should we know?' Then with teeth-grating inevitability, 'We are not God.'

The schoolteacher, a chubby Christian, flashed his authoritative glasses. 'Death? I can tell you about death. It's all in the Bible, the Word of God. We are told we must spread the Word of God.' I groaned. The gloom was going to be made complete. It was back to Sunday School.

61

'No,' I said, hoping to stem the flow. 'I mean a story of the old people.'

'Yes, yes. The old people. Adam and Eve.' And he was off. 'In those days, only Adam and Eve lived in a big field. There was everything they needed. No weeds grew. They did not have to plant and hoe. No rats ate their crops. The millet came up like the razor grass and the heads dropped off with no work. They needed no threshing songs. They never had to move the field. In the middle was a big tree and a strong spirit lived in it. God told them not to annoy the spirit by stealing the fruit of the tree – like the mango trees at the mission, but it was a *tarko* tree. But the chameleon came and –'

'Snake,' I said. 'Surely you mean snake?'

'There were no snakes in that field!' he snapped. 'Everything in the world was kind and good. It was the chameleon that still changes its colour to deceive men.'

He put on a little squeaky voice to represent the chameleon. The men laughed. ' "Oh Eve," ' he said, waggling his behind. ' "I'm so hungry and I walk so slowly. Won't you put me on that tree so I can eat?" Eve was afraid. "God told me to stay away from the *tarko* tree," she said. But the chameleon persuaded her with its honey tongue and she put it on the tree and it gave her some fruit to eat.' The schoolteacher made a face; *tarko* is very bitter. 'Then she saw she was naked and made herself clothes of leaves like the women still wear. And she cooked Adam a sauce of *tarko* and he ate it and right away he looked at her and they had sex Pow! right there, and he had to wear leaves like men still do at death.' He paused for breath, then rustled round the hut, bandy-legged, in simulated leaves and bent down in a way that would have exposed his backside. They screamed and clapped.

'Then God came.' Deep voice now. ' "What's this? You have disobeyed." And he beat them so men still get lines on their foreheads where they were struck. "For this you will have children one at a time instead of all together like the animals." Then God made rocks in the world and thorns and weeds and death.'

That was really quite interesting. Surprising really. It was under the *tarko* tree that circumcision was invented. 'About the *tarko*...' I began.

'Then they had two sons Cain and Abel and Cain was a good man who grew millet and Abel kept goats. Abel's children became the Fulani.'

'Ah,' the men nodded. So that was it. The Fulani who drifted with their livestock over the Dowayo fields in the dry season.

'And Cain had sons who became us and others blacksmiths and hunters. But Abel's animals ravaged all the crops Cain had planted in the rocks and the thorns and the weeds and when he complained Abel just laughed. He just laughed,' he repeated and shook his head at the wonder of it. 'So Cain killed him Thud! So now we live with blacksmiths and others but always fight with the Fulani because of that old grudge.'

Enthusiastic applause, slapping of hands on thighs. This was far too good not to dig further.

'And Europeans?' I asked. 'White men like myself. Where did they come from?'

'He appraised me coolly. 'I have studied the Bible in great depth, monsieur. As far as I recall, there are no white men in it.'

Death is such an important event that most cultures encapsulate it in myth and ritual, give it at least a place in the world if not a justification. Is death inevitable, part of Nature, part of a balanced universe? Or is it all a subsequent error, an unintended intrusion of disorder into order? The Christian myth of Genesis prepares us for the second view with death only emerging as primal purity falls apart. It is assumed that mortality comes as part of a deadly package defining the human character through free will and enterprise that emerge in the form of sin, knowledge and sex. As human fertility appears, the spontaneous fertility of the soil is reduced and, henceforth, the harvesting of food will involve labour. The myth belongs to a worldwide group of stories involving death as the result of a violated interdiction or as the price to be paid for social and sexual life. But here the Bible itself is unsatisfactorily vague. Offstage, there is talk of a tree of life that would have granted Adam immortality and is therefore kept from him. The Old Saxon translation has two trees, one of good, one of evil; while the apple of folklore is the fruit of false etymology, Latin neuter *malum*, 'evil', having the same form as the accusative *malum*, meaning 'apple', the Fang of the Congo have reworked the myth through their own language and here the forbidden fruit is *ebon*, a word that besides designating a particular fruit also means 'vagina'.

On the Indonesian island of Roti, where life centres about the sugary sap of the lontar palm, other changes have been made. The Rotinese poem of the origin of death attributes it not to consumption of an apple but of lontar fruit:

If you pick the fruit of the syrup tree
Or if you pluck the leaf of the honey tree
There is sourness there
A spirit of death lies there
There is bitterness there . . .*

The upshot of it all is that the lontar tree is cut down to become a coffin for Mankind, a usage that continues to this day. Knowledge, sin and death come in a single container.

Many myths show Man not just falling prey to death but actually seeking it out and buying it like a rare thing, a solution to the problems of life. The myth creates a question to which death is the answer. The Samo of Burkina Faso have a view that all disturbances of natural order, death included, have the same primal cause:

*Fox, 1983

When Men lived in the sky they did not die. Since there were getting too many, God, helped by the blacksmith, sent a certain number of them to the earth where they organised themselves into two groups – the Masters of the Earth who reigned over cold and dry and the Masters of Rain who reigned over heat and humidity. So the world was completely balanced: when the Masters of Rain increased the heat, this caused drought on earth; then the Masters of the Earth increased the humidity to unleash the rain. For the same reasons of balance, the Masters of Rain, fated to die, had no contact with their own dead and the Masters of the Earth, who were immortal, worked as gravediggers. The former were content with their lot and made no complaint; when one of them died, they organised the funeral ceremonies and ate the *lalso* [a dish prepared by the female lineage members of the deceased]. But the Masters of the Earth were jealous; they too wanted to eat the *lalso*. So they sent two messengers into the bush to buy Death for the price of a cat. They finally got it for a cow and became the equals of the Masters of Rain. It was too bad that the harmony of the world was disturbed; in fact from then on Men had to allow for the unpredictability of the seasons, drought and bad harvests: that was the real price you had to pay for life.*

There is a curious disproportion about death. Often it is the result of an apparently trivial event that deflects the world from its course, like a science-fiction story in which a time traveller treads on a butterfly with terrible consequences. It comes from a jumping contest between a frog and a toad, or an animal stopping to have a snack, or a child's naughtiness, or an old woman testily telling God to get out of her way. Sometimes a single wrong choice unleashes death.

The Dyula of Senegal tell that God created the first man and gave him a wife. It goes on: 'One day, he called them and showed them two bags. The bigger one was stuffed with presents, foodstuffs and utilitarian goods. It also contained death. The smaller one contained immortality. "Which one will you choose?" God asked. The man hesitated but the woman insisted on getting the

*Heritier–Izard, 1973:243

goods. So they took the bag and carried it away. And since then, all men must die.'*

The same myth occurs among the Ngala of the Upper Congo but with an added refinement. Here, the bundle contains beads, knives, cloth and looking-glasses – all exotic imports. So the woman is not just choosing wealth but trade and contact with the outside world i.e. social life.

In some cases, death may come as a punishment for folly or sin or over-reaching oneself. The Asante of Ghana tell that:

> A long time ago, the heavenly god was very close to Men. The mother of these men, while pounding *fufu*, kept knocking him with her pestle. To avoid the blows, God shifted higher up. So the woman ordered her sons to pile up all the mortars to be closer to God. They obeyed but were one mortar short to be high enough. Their mother told them to take the mortar from the bottom of the pile. They did so and the tower collapsed and killed many of them. That's how death came among Men.[†]

The Luba of Zaire have a story more closely paralleling that of the Bible:

> God had many bananas. He picked them and buried them so they would ripen. Later, he sent the sun, then the moon and stars to dig them up and bring them to him. He asked each of them if they had eaten any. They said no and it was true. Then he sent Man. Man dug them up, looked at them for a long time and said to himself, 'Even if I eat some, father will not know because there are a lot.' He took one, found it to be delicious and swallowed several. He took the rest back to his father's house. God asked him, 'Have you tasted them?' 'Absolutely not,' said Man. 'If you haven't eaten any, I'll send you back again tomorrow.' The next day, Man tried to get up and go to greet his father. His legs felt wobbly. God waited for him in vain, then went to Man. 'Why are you lying down?' he asked him. Man didn't

*Thomas, 1982:27
[†]Thomas, 1982:32

66

move and didn't know what to say. God continued, 'You have certainly eaten some of the bananas, otherwise you would not be ill!' Having said thus, God departed. Man remained stretched out, became more and more ill and died. Death has stayed always amongst us on account of the theft by the first man. The sun, moon and stars have stayed beautiful as God made them. And we are left to die, to die.*

With true ethnographic insight, the Bible has murder invented by Cain and Abel and ever since the sociological view has seen mortality as reflecting the tensions of family life. We are murdered by our loved ones. According to the Kiga of Uganda:

In the beginning, men suddenly got young again when they were becoming too old or else they died and revived some time afterwards. One day an old woman died and was buried. Her daughter-in-law who detested her secretly went to the cemetery and watched the tomb, waiting for the soil to rise up. When it did, she thudded her pestle down on the soil and shouted, 'The dead shouldn't come back.' The mother-in-law never did come back. But from then on, those who died no longer revived.†

———❧———

It is newly fashionable to see death and decline as intimately linked to the faults that occur in the copying of DNA in cell replication. This is just a reworking of an old motif – the message that failed. In Africa, death is often the result of a garbled or misdirected message.

In East Africa, it is the hare who acts as the messenger and gets things the wrong way round so that Man ends up dying. In West Africa, it is more often the chameleon. So according to the Bamun of Cameroon:

*Thomas, 1982:35
†Thomas, 1982:38

One day the chameleon and the toad began to discuss the fate of
Men. The toad thought Men should die temporarily, then come to
life again. The chameleon maintained they should die once and for
all. To decide the affair, the toad suggested they announce the news
by beating a drum placed an agreed distance away. The first to reach
the drum would beat out its own message. The chameleon knew the
toad was fond of winged termites. During the night it set three lots of
them on the route, one at the start, the second in the middle, the third
near the end. The toad lost a lot of time swallowing them and the
chameleon arrived first. That's why men die.*

This is also the reason people give nowadays for their horror of the
sluggish chameleon and the frequent injunction to kill it by stuff-
ing its mouth with snuff.

A common symbol of immortality is the snake, able to slough its
skin and so rejuvenate itself. This provides mythic thought with
another way of placing the condition of men in contrast with animals as a way of elaborating a more complete scheme of Nature.
According to the Chaga of Uganda:

> In the beginning, men admittedly got old but went through a con-
> tinuous process of rejuvenation and shed their skin as the snake still
> does. One day a mother sent her child to the river. While she was
> away, she intended to slough off her skin and be rejuvenated. The
> child returned, however, sooner than expected and surprised her in
> the act of slipping out of her skin. So, the transformation remained
> incomplete and the mother died in her old skin.†

Or humans and animals can be identified. The Lui of Zambia tell
that the culture hero Nyambe formerly lived on earth together
with his wife Nasilele. 'His dog died and he desired it back; but his
wife considered that the dog was a thief, and should be thrown
out. This was done. But also Nasilele's mother died, and now she

*Rein-Wuhrmann, 1925:139
†Gutmann, 1909:123

wished her mother to be restored to life. Nyambe refused, since he had not got his dog back.*

The Dan of the Ivory Coast point out the similarity between men as hunters of animals and Death as the hunter of men:

> A young man went hunting in the forest. In those days, Death, who only killed animals, was also in the forest. Up until then, no one had seen him. On a fire, the young man saw an animal that Death had set to cook, then met Death in the forest. Death said, 'Come here! You're a hunter like me. We're alike.' The hunter stayed with Death for several days. Death gave him meat. The hunter said thank you and brought some pieces back to the village. But he did not know he had assumed a debt. One day, Death came to the village and said, 'Pay me what you owe me.' Then the hunter said, 'So it wasn't a present but a loan?' Death declared, 'I was in the forest. You came and took all my meat. You must pay me back!' The hunter said, 'Right, take one of my children!' Immediately, Death seized one of the children.[†]

—◦◦◦—

Often myths play with time and the different sorts of regeneration found in Nature. Time affects men differently from other elements of the world, as in a Liberian myth:

> An old man just back from a far country tells of a medicine-man there was 'savvy too much for them sick palaver.' They beg the old man to go and find the medicine-man and bring a medicine . . . to cure the sick and revive the dead. The old man refuses. He says, 'I am too old, and the country too far for me to go again. Let us send Cat. He is swift and his life be plenty strong.' They agree and Cat sets out. He finds Medicine-Man and persuades him to prepare his most potent medicine. 'Guard it well, friend Cat! It will cure the sick and revive the dead,' cautions Medicine-Man. On his way back, Cat comes to a

*Abrahamsson, 1951:65
[†]Paulme, 1978

river. It is hot and Cat is weary. He will bathe. He lays the medicine down on the stump of a tree on the bank. Coming out of the water, he forgets the medicine, and hastens home. He tells the people of his success; but, on looking for the medicine, he cannot find it, and remembers where he left it. The people beat him, and drive him forth to recover the medicine. When he reaches the stump by the river, the medicine is gone. He runs to Medicine-Man who is outraged by his carelessness. Medicine-Man says that through the stump the medicine has crept into the boat and cannot be recovered. Henceforward, although a tree be cut, if the stump remain, the tree will grow again; but when men die it will be the end.*

Hans Abrahamsson has collected many African myths of this type. Among the Bongo of Sudan a message is sent that men shall die and come back like the moon that shall live for ever.[†] But the wrong message gets delivered. Among the Kongo of the Congo the first man to die goes to Heaven in the rainy season and receives two leaves, a wet and a dry one i.e. a sign on earth they shall both live and die like the seasons.[‡] The Acoli of Sudan say that men originally became old and were buried but grew back like plants at the new moon, or slept but awoke young.** Other choices on offer are to live like the moon (i.e. be reborn) or like the banana (i.e. to live on through offspring since the banana must be cut down to regrow new shoots every season).

Exactly the same concerns occur in South America as shown in Levi-Strauss's M76 Shipaya myth:

The demiurge wished to make men immortal. He told them to take up their position at the water's edge and to allow two canoes to go by; they should, however, stop the third in order to greet and embrace the spirit in it.

*Bundy, 1919:408
[†]Abrahamsson, 1951:13
[‡]Abrahamsson, 1951:14
**Abrahamsson, 1951:16

The first canoe contained a basket full of rotten meat, which was extremely foul smelling. The men ran toward it but were repelled by the stench. They thought that this canoe was carrying death, whereas death was in the second canoe and had taken human form. As a result, men greeted death warmly, with embraces. When the demiurge arrived in the third canoe, he had to accept the fact that the men had chosen death – unlike the snakes, the trees and the stones, who had all awaited the arrival of the spirit of immortality. Had men done likewise, they would have sloughed off their skins when they grew old, and would have become young again like snakes.*

Similar basic themes are found in the rituals of the Tlingit Indians of Alaska. There was widespread opposition between the wet and impermanent and the dry and eternal. Rites involved using rocks and stones to weigh down the clothes of pubescent girls to steady them and prevent them dying young. Raven, the creator god, it was said, had tried to make men out of rock which made them eternal but failed as it also made them slow. So he used leaf, making men swift but condemning them to age and die like plants.

The same concerns with the placing of change and death can be expressed through pictures. Recently, a friend of mine attended a family funeral. She belonged to what she called a 'family by correspondence', one of those that keep in touch by phonecalls, postcards from remote places, computer-produced newsletters. Since the deceased was the last member of his generation, many felt obliged to turn up who, despite close kinship, seldom – if ever – actually met. Cousins had to be introduced and their kinship links untangled. Older relatives checked each other for the ravages of time. They took a group photograph outside the church to the horrified protests of the vicar. 'This is not', he cried stepping, appalled, into shot with hands over face, 'a happy occasion.'

Photographs – as advertisements assure us – 'eternalize the

*Levi-Strauss, 1970:155

moment.' In the West, to do so at a wedding is good; to do so at a funeral is bad. Death is the fate that dare not show its face. In the most photo-loving of Western cultures, America, the rouged and lipsticked corpse itself, surrounded by flowers in the slumber room, is the 'Living Memory Picture' and photographs of it are discouraged.

Other cultures do not see things in the same way. Group photos at West Indian funerals celebrate the solidarity of the surviving family. In Java, it is normal to snap family and friends looking down on the corpse with a 'tenseless expression' on the faces, approximating that on the face of dead.* Most family albums include pictures of dead bodies. Indeed, it has been argued that the Javanese lack of hysteria about corpses is due to their belief that the dead provide an acceptable image of ideal behaviour for the living – paragons of still, unengaged aloofness. The curious sadness of Italian cemeteries seems to lie precisely in those fading sepia photographs of the dead incorporated in the headstones. So datable and evocative of the past, they undermine their own attempt to declare that time has been stopped in its tracks.

Photographs are stored in albums that 'record' the course of a life but they do not record objectively. Instead, like one anthropological view of ritual, they construct a fictitious account of triumphs and successes where everyone always smiles. Like obituaries they are forgeries of the memory. In the Western album, the last scene, the funeral, is always missing.

In Western views of life, death is not included. 'Death by old age' is no longer an acceptable cause to write on the certificate; a disease must be found so that no death is counted truly inevitable. We see lives as stories. In the history of other cultures, it is striking how often it is an anthropologist's assistant who writes the first autobiography in the local language. Philippe Aries has plotted the way in which book-keeping creeps into Christian notions of judgement in the twelfth and thirteenth centuries until a person's guardian angel ends up with a 'This Is Your Life' book to be pre-

*Siegel, 1983

72

sented after death that delivers the deceased's life for judgement.*

In our narratives, it is frequently only the end that gives meaning, that casts a retrospective significance over all the seemingly haphazard events that led up to it. In detective fiction, the fact that the under-gardener repotted the begonias at two o'clock precisely is not – we now see – trivial. In the light of the ending, this fact is transformed and enables us to untangle the whole mystery and find the hidden, hitherto obscured, pattern. It is therefore not surprising that Western anthropologists have sought, in funerary practice, the sense of an ending that would solve and interpret all the vicissitudes of life.

Some cultures seem to fit this model. A Chinese funeral traditionally began with the announcement of the death in printed form. This included genealogical information, the achievements and offices held by the deceased and a list of his honours, virtues etc. Even in modern newspaper versions of these a similar pattern is followed, including lists of the names of relatives of different categories.

Traditionally, these would be plumped out with incidents blatantly lifted from classical tales, such as the one telling how a doting son, in order to cure an ailing parent, sliced off part of his own body to add to the medicine. The age of the deceased would be exaggerated to add to his honour. The final tomb would incorporate a plaque naming the deceased's ancestors and descendants. Often these would be largely fictitious, sometimes entirely so.

Our own urge to see life in narrative terms is clear in the creation of heroes whose lives must fit into an acceptable narrative form with alternative endings to please different factions. So Catholic propagandists rewrote the death of the great agnostic Voltaire to have him either calling out for forgiveness or eating his own excrement.

Horatio Nelson, whose end occurred at the moment of his greatest triumph, is actually better thanatological material than Napoleon despite all the latter's undoubted achievements. He sim-

*Aries, 1981

ply lived too long and suffered what amounts to a seedy seaside retirement in drastically reduced circumstances. Little wonder that French historians seek constantly to suggest that he was poisoned and so transform his dull, domestic end into a dramatic English murder.

———*ᴏᴏᴏ*———

The Kraho of Venezuela refer to photos as *mekaro*. They use the same word for something like 'soul', 'spirit', 'ghost' – an enduring principle that lives on after death.* The usage recalls the lingering Victorian belief that invisible ghosts could be captured in photographs but the term does not seem to rest on any idea that the 'soul' is trapped by the film. Rather it is that a photograph 'freezes' life. For death among the Kraho involves journeying to a world that punishes men by giving them that which they most earnestly desire.

In some ways it is simply a reverse of this world: nocturnal, favouring shade instead of sunlight. More importantly, it is a world without outsider wives, that most disruptive element of social life, a world where men and their kin can live together instead of moving in with unrelated women as they must on earth. Yet, because it is closed, its peace is that of total sterility expressed by the village centring not on the dynamic public square but a pond of stagnant water. The 'souls' go through various transformations – the actual number varies from informant to informant – but end up as motionless stones or tree roots, as in the myths above, and pay the price of permanence by losing all social life.

The American moonshots of the 1970s were a triumphal statement of the power of applied science and pragmatic materialism. The proposal to fire the bodies of the dead into space raises the

*Carneiro da Cunha, 1981

74

symbolic power of technology to poetry, an overcoming of the limitations of the physical by contact with the sacralising power of science. There is no reason that technology cannot become myth and we often hop happily from one myth to another, in spite of their being of quite contradictory import. Hence we also have the Frankenstein story that argues the perils of overweening human faith in science.

In South America, it is common knowledge that the spaceshots only succeeded because of the literal crushing of the bodies of poor people. From the ritual murder of the Peruvian poor and the processing of their bodies, the Americans extracted the 'grease' that is essential for metallurgy, pharmaceuticals and the lubrication of the moon rockets.[*] The story goes that the simple traveller is attacked in remote places by the *nakaq*, a demonic creature in the form of a bearded white man, wearing a white poncho, riding a white mule and carrying a machete. Or sometimes, he is a mestizo wearing the flayed skin of his victims and riding a black mule. Sometimes he is both at the same time.

He lurks on lonely roads, slashes his victims' throats and hangs them up in mineshafts so that the bodies drip their fat into vessels. Occasionally, he uses a powder made of foetuses, extracted from the female dead, to dull their wits. He is able to flense the fat from the living bodies in a mystical operation so that the travellers are able to continue to their destination where, unaware of their ordeal, they rapidly weaken and die.

A secondary elaboration sees the Catholic Church as issuing licences to such *nakaqs* to cull its congregation.[†] This neatly explains such diverse phenomena as priestly interference with traditional death rituals and the observed commonness of autopsies in Church hospitals. The sanctuary lamp, of course, runs on human grease which is also used for the casting of Church bells.

Others have broadened the scope of the belief and expanded it to the point where they see the whole state as ultimately financed

*Gose, 1986
†Casaverde, 1970

by these operations, and the process has been readily interpretable as an allegory of the peasant view of the global commodity market and his own exploited place within it. Or it can represent the parasitic relationship of city and countryside. Or state and citizen. Or industrialization and agriculture.

Political interpretations of death myths have long been appetizing to Western intellectuals. The Dracula myth with its pale, aristocratic vampire lowering himself on to submissive maids ripe with fresh blood has been a ready candidate for interpretation as a tale of upper-class sexual exploitation of peasant women.

Yet the grease myth is not new, nor even a product of the nineteenth century. Already in the 1560s the central components were in place and being recorded by puzzled Spanish writers. In the twentieth century it has been adopted by the Shining Path Maoist guerillas and harnessed to the propaganda of the modern age. The Path is, after all, headed by an academic, Chairman Gonzalo, apparently greatly influenced by the research of anthropologists.* The enemies of the Path are identified with the *nakaqs* and everyone knows that *nakaqs* must be killed and hideously mutilated to prevent their return.

*Strong, 1993

4

The Quick and the Dead: Relations across the Grave

' Why should the generations overlap one another at all? Why cannot
we be buried as eggs in neat little cells with ten or twenty thousand
pounds each wrapped round us in Bank of England notes, and wake
up, as the sphex wasp does, to find that its papa and mamma have not
only left ample provision at its elbow, but have been eaten by sparrows
some weeks before it began to live consciously on its own account?'
Samuel Butler, *The Way of All Flesh,* 1903

Samuel Butler assumed that you have no social relationship with
previous generations. In most of the world this is not so. In the
literature on the living and the dead, there is frequent talk of 'sacrifices', 'offerings' and 'worship'. When freshly arrived in Africa,
I saw a boy screaming insults into the air just down the hill from
the mission. 'You greedy bastards,' he shouted, tears running down
his face. 'We gave you beer. We gave you a cow. Stop making So-
and-So ill. Leave us alone. Clear off! I don't care if you kill me too.
Go ahead. Then I'll really get you, you bastards.'

'What is he doing?' I asked the priest. 'Is he shouting at the
mission?'

'Oh, no,' he replied suavely, 'that's ancestor worship. And he's
lying about the cow. He never gave it.'

It is normally impossible to distinguish between lies and symbolism. A Chinese friend once told me that he had offered a
pig to the dead. 'A whole pig?' I asked, somewhat surprised,

since I knew he was far from being a rich man. He laughed. 'No. We fool them. What we do is offer the head and the tail, maybe the feet. Then they fill in the blanks and assume we gave the rest too.'

So the grovelling postures of Christians at worship are only one form of interaction with spirits. They can be cajoled, threatened and cheated. An Avatip (New Guinea) man expressed it more bluntly, 'We would beat up our ancestral ghosts, if only they were visible to us.'*

(In all of this 'worshippers' remind an ethnographer of nothing so much as fellow Western academics. You have only to look at the hosts of dead forebears listed in their bibliographies to realize that they − whatever their proclaimed religions − are ancestor worshippers. And their behaviour towards those forebears is not unlike that of many Africans towards their dead.)

Anthropologists from Durkheim on have stressed the somewhat rough-and-ready correspondences implied by the former's statement that 'Religion is society writ large.' The sorts of correspondences they have in mind are those in which Australian aborigines pair off groups of men and groups of animals as their ancestors. Or the way Mediterranean cultures approach God through local saints in the form of celestial fixers and middlemen, just as they approach political power through local *padrones*. Or the way the Kingdom of God has entered into the theory and justification of monarchy and vice versa, for the next world can serve as a model for this one and if there is too much of a gap between them it is sometimes *this* world that will have to be changed. Human beings do not always take the easiest path.

By a similar correspondence, individualist cultures have either slain God or rendered him impotent. A turning point in the West was the decline of the notion of Purgatory after the Reformation. Those on this side − family, friends, whatever − could no longer affect the fate of those that had gone before; nor could the dead do anything to affect the lot of the living. Each man henceforth kept

*Harrison, 1993

his own balance sheet and the next world could then begin to wither away.

In the study of funeral customs, Madagascar, with its wealth of different funerary practices, has become a sort of natural laboratory for exploring such ideas. A typical example would be that of Maurice Bloch who relates differences in burial arrangements and variations in social organisation.*

The dominant Merina group see a profound unity between people and land. They construct stone and cement tombs for the dead that contrast with the flimsy dwellings of the living. After all, death is for eternity. People should marry within their own group and anyone dying away must be brought back to their place of origin for burial. In jolly ceremonies called *famadihana*, they take out the bodies, dance with them, talk to them, possibly take them around the area to show them recent changes, and rewrap them before putting them back in the tomb. There is music, singing and dancing. One tune noted at such events is 'Roll Out the Barrel'.[†] The emphasis is on the grinding up and mixing of bodies so that they again form a unity that overcomes individuation. There is a fair amount of freedom in choosing which tomb you will actually be buried in but a firm commitment must be made to the big social and financial costs of membership of a tomb group. So where you will be buried determines who your closest allies are in life and vice versa.

The Sakalava of the west coast, on the other hand, were traditionally an alliance of rather varied peoples. Royal men took wives from subject groups and produced royal children. Royal women were impregnated by a male concubine, not a husband, so that the children from these unions were also royal. Gradually more and more people ended up royal.

Whenever a king dies, his spirit is expected to enter into a living person. This person must be found, brought to the capital and adopt the regalia of the deceased monarch. At *his* death, a replace-

*Bloch, 1981
[†]Mack, 1986: 76

ment is found and so on, with the result that all the kings that ever were are held still to be in the capital. While commoner tombs may be rather grand affairs, royal bodies are housed in somewhat drab structures – since the kings themselves are held not to have died. Over time, more and more people end up inside the tomb-village and it becomes a ritual focus of the emerging state. So the royal group swallows up commoners as the tomb swallows up subjects.

'It is easier for a camel to pass through the eye of a needle than for a rich man to enter the Kingdom of Heaven.' Culturally, this is not one of Christianity's most exportable notions. It's not just specific, foot-notey problems – that the eye of a needle is supposed to be a notoriously narrow city gate in Jerusalem or that Eskimos don't have camels. Notions of the everyday afterlife may too closely reflect the conditions of this world for us to imagine a place where wealth counts against you. Concerning Africa, Jean-Vincent Thomas has remarked: 'If to die is to become a spirit, it is astonishing that the next life is described in such realist terms that it is the replica of this lower world, with the same needs, the same social hierarchies and the same passions.'*

Muslim orthodoxy concentrates rather on the fate of the male than the female but seems to see the afterlife as a place where there is no labour or hardship: '. . . The true servants of God shall be well provided for, feasting on fruit and honoured in the gardens of delight. Reclining face to face upon soft couches, they shall be served with a goblet filled at a gushing fountain, white, and delicious to those who drink it. It will neither dull their senses nor befuddle them. They shall sit with bashful, dark-eyed virgins, as chaste as the sheltered eggs of ostriches.'†

The proof that Westerners have largely ceased to believe in a credible paradise is that it is not popularly pictured as an eternal fortnight in Torremolinos for it is nowadays only in our holidays

*Thomas, 1982:129
†Koran, 37:25

80

that our own threadbare notions of a heavenly existence are to be found. Modern Christian theologians are unusual in their unwillingness to describe the next life that they hold out as a prize. Significantly, slippery negatives play a disproportionate part in such details as they give. Heaven is *not* this, *not* that.

The Bobo of Burkina Faso have an almost Kafkaesque view of eternity, drawing on their experience of the world as a heavily maladministered place where documents are regularly checked by importunate officials, and tax receipts must be produced on demand.* The ancestors are a sort of bureaucratic border police. The newly dead must wait to cross the River Volta to become ancestors themselves. Meanwhile, their credentials are suspiciously examined at great length to check that expensive and intricate rituals have been carried out correctly by the living.

To the Chinese, the adaptation of the soul to its new and complex environment in hell is a matter of the primest importance. This hell is, in its administrative aspects, rather like another China 'ploughed under', with a similar complicated system of rewards, punishments and financial obligations on the part of the soul. Ransom payments must be made to the ruler of Hades to procure rebirth under circumstances most propitious for a successful and prosperous life; 'squeeze' money must be given to judges, *pour boire* to hungry ghosts, and certificates owned (burnt for one by one's relatives) to enable one to pass any barrier encountered on one's wanderings there. A soul in hell without the financial support of the living would be in an unenviable position. Paper houses, sedan chairs and automobiles, trunks of clothes and other adjuncts to good living together with quantities of mock money of various kinds must be burnt for its comfort or what little comfort it can find between the almost continuous tortures suffered in the Chinese Hades. Everything burnt must be of the best possible quality: a poor quality paper house, as one paper image maker told us, would scarcely last out to the end of the hundred days of mourning activities. So the expense involved in settlement in the new land is often considerable.†

*Le Moal, 1989
†Topely, 1952:148–59

81

Since this was written, the Chinese afterworld has kept pace with the changes of this one. In the old days, you would send paper cut-outs of servants. Nowadays, offerings include paper steam irons, vacuum cleaners, credit cards, compact-disc-players, computers, fans and motorbikes – all the trivial paraphernalia of mortal existence. This is a next world that seems depressingly familar, sordidly material, where the breakdown of the washing machine is still a major nuisance, offering no vision of escape to a more spiritual plane. While utilitarian goods can be easily shunted across the next world by burning them, dough cakes and sticks will be placed directly in the coffin. These are not there as aids to a hungry, tired, wayfaring ghost. Their function is quite specific. Because vicious dogs are known to haunt the outer marches of Hell they are to be used to alternatively distract or beat off the beasts.

The relations between this world and the next are thus the reverse of those postulated by the Shakers. This sect, founded by Ann Lee in mid-eighteenth-century England and exported to America, would receive spiritual – therefore invisible – objects from the other world. At meetings, the Shakers would eat untasteable heavenly fruit and march to the playing of invisible and inaudible muscial instruments.

Yet, it is easy to impose a false coherence on other people's ideas of the essentially numinous relations between the worlds. Below the simple level of Chinese practice, all is disorder. The Chinese notion of the complementary polarities *yin* and *yang* urges us to distinguish a *yin* soul, that goes into the grave, from a *yang* soul that ends up on the ancestral tablet. Ritual practice suggests three souls with another going to the underworld. Traditional number symbolism interacts with this system to produce no less than three *yin* and seven *yang* souls. Regional variation, an indigenous theocracy and an overlay of Western interpretation have all made their contributions to produce what is now a position of total incoherence in 'Chinese beliefs concerning the afterworld'.

Even within the relative uniformity of African notions of the hereafter, there is some variation, especially where the bad dead – those who suffer an 'unnatural' death – are concerned. Often they are held to walk backwards or upside down, to wear their clothes back to front, to be nocturnal, or white-skinned or left-handed, in a simple reversal of that which is normal in this world.

Reversal is a common way of imagining an unknown world. In the eighteenth century, Richard Hull had himself buried under a tower on Leith Hill. He insisted on being interred on horseback and upside down in the belief that this would be to his advantage on Judgement Day when again the world would be reversed and he alone would then be the right way up.

Jacques Meunier urges us more generally to caution when moving from interpretation of rituals of death to the world of life. 'Is it possible,' he asks, 'starting from a scrapyard, to reconstruct the Highway Code?'*

Indeed, certain regional styles intrude to complicate the idea that the next world is either just like this one or this one on its head. Some peoples such as the Oceanic Tikopians have a whole range of somewhat frivolous designer-afterworlds, some reserved for one-legged people, others for cannibals, some built on a slant so that they can tip over and dump the unwary. These are not taken very seriously. South America seems to see the afterlife above all as a sort of adventure playground in which to try out all sorts of weird and wonderful forms of social organization. Joanna Overing has shown how the Piaroa of Venezuela create for their dead a complex system of groupings that looks totally foreign and pointless when seen from their life on this side but recalls the organization of other outsider groups with which they are acquainted.[†] It is as if we should decide to imagine the afterworld as like the Russian army – credible but problematic.

*Meunier, 1994
†Overing, 1993

Crematoria these days are so busy that the average ceremony takes less than fifteen minutes. As one coffin trundles down the ramp, another is being lugged through the door, feet first – always feet first unless it's a priest when it goes head first. After all, in church he always faced the other way from the congregation. Outside, the hearses are circling like aeroplanes stacked over a major airport. Beneath, the chapel is a light industrial plant for the processing of identity to dust with the industrial overtones carefully hidden. Only Hindu mourners penetrate down here, the Christians stay upstairs with the ecclesiastical atmosphere and the rose garden. For Hindus, the funeral pyre should ideally be lit by the eldest son, and nowadays he is permitted to go where others may not to press the start button on the furnace.

All around, signs warn of the dire professional consequences should the hydraulic hoist emit groans. The furnace door stands open and, silhouetted against the flames as in some joke of hellfire, there is a priest. I ask about the groans.

'Well', he offers cheerfully, 'you wouldn't want people having any last-minute doubts. In fact,' he confides, 'sometimes we give the coffin a last check before we pop the body in the furnace. It's not that any of them are going to be alive – not after having the blood sucked out of their hearts with a steel tube. It's self-preservation. Normally the coffins are closed but you get the occasional open one still. People are always dropping last little things in. They seem to see it as a journey to a foreign country where you may not be able to get some of the things you have here. I've seen the widow slide in a packet of his favourite digestive biscuits. Or it's the spare glasses and the set of false teeth. You wouldn't believe how many tubes of dental fixative go through here in a week. Old people always think of that. They know the hell of being without. But it's other things you have to worry about. A few years back we had an explosion that bent the furnace door. It was the widow. She'd popped a couple of cans of some spray adhesive the departed used to paste on his toupee. It went up with a bang that nearly took the lot of us with it. It's about love, you see. What can you give someone they can really use when they're dead?'

The objects assigned to the grave with the dead are worthy of a whole study in themselves. Indeed, they already have one – without them, classical archaeology is unthinkable. Grave goods may include sumptuous finery, untold wealth in gold and precious gems, food, money, weapons, horses and even servants.

Two lines of thought are common where intimate possessions are concerned. Their link with the dead may turn them into inalienable heirlooms or relics, kept by the living as witness to a bond between themselves and the departed. This connection may well be physically impregnated into the object as the 'fine patina of use' so beloved of auction houses. Alternatively, some objects may be *too* closely associated with the dead and must be consigned to the grave, sometimes broken or 'killed', to appear over the other side. Robert Hertz, the theoretician of death, extends this process to the body itself.* As it rots in this world, it reappears in the next.

The different decisions made by different cultures about what is to go and what to stay constitute much of the raw material by which we know the past. Many of our most basic assumptions about ancient cultures are questionable. In excavations, it is common sense to classify the distribution of different sorts of grave goods according to the sex and age of the body they are found with. However, powerful women, or those past menopause, may in some cases be classified and buried as 'male'; uncircumcised or unmarried men may be classed as 'children' or 'female'.

Pottery – the absolute staple of archaeology – is important here too. The breaking of pots in and on the grave may have all sorts of implications. They may be seen by outside interpreters as functional goods needed by the dead. But they are more likely to be distinguishing different sorts of people through their association with different sorts of pots. Among the Sirak of North Cameroon, the grave of a woman who has many children is marked with a pot normally used to store flour, while the sort of eating bowl used by a man is smashed on the tomb of a

*Hertz, 1907

85

leper.* The needs of the dead are hardly involved in such choices.

In parts of Madagascar a transistor radio is placed beside the body. Just before the grave is closed over it, the radio is switched on as in a Duracell battery advertisement.

Such acts seem deceptively transparent but do not necessarily translate easily into beliefs about the material needs of the dead or any surviving spirit. In a move that would drive archaeologists to distraction, pilgrims to the grave of Andy Warhol have taken to stacking it with unopened cans of Campbell's soup.

—◈◈◈—

> The same day came unto him the Sadducees, which say that there is no resurrection, and asked him saying, Master, Moses said, If a man die, having no children, his brother shall marry his wife, and raise up seed unto his brother. Now there were with us seven brethren: and the first, when he had married a wife, deceased, and, having no issue, left his wife unto his brother: likewise the second also, and the third, unto the seventh. And last of all the woman died also. Therefore in the resurrection whose wife shall be of the seven? For they all had her. Jesus answered and said unto them, Ye do err, not knowing the scriptures, nor the power of God. For in the resurrection they neither marry, nor are given in marriage, but are as the angels of God in heaven . . .   Matthew 22:23–31

Other cultures would not agree. We tend to regard death as effecting a kind of divorce. Hollywood movies, such as the very successful *Ghost* or *Dying Young*, delight in showing that the individual dead live and love on. But this is not the social bond of marriage; this is the Western obsession with romantic love which triumphs over all, even death. In *Wuthering Heights*, Heathcliffe bribes the sexton to slip his coffin in beside that of his beloved Catherine despite the inconvenient existence of her husband. And

*Sterner, 1989

not for nothing are the heroes of pop culture those who have died before ageing and institutional marriage.

We are familiar with the Hindu practice of *sutee*, where the links between husband and wife are held to be so strong that a widow might immolate herself on her husband's funeral pyre, and with the Mediterranean usage where a widow remains married to her late husband, goes into black on his death, and remarriage is as unthinkable as divorce. In imperial China, the greatest praise was reserved for a wife who arranged to hang herself publicly on the death of her spouse and the event would be graced by the presence of local dignitaries. Such deaths were not regarded as suicide but as a heroic victory over death.

In much of Africa, death does not dissolve the bonds that link the families of those involved. On the death of her husband, a woman may be assigned to his son or brother and even if this does not happen any children born to her may still belong to them. Sometimes different forms of marriage produce a different degree of incorporation of the spouse. Whether or not a dead wife's bones are returned to the place where she was born may depend on the bride price paid. Among the Nigerian Ijaw, if a high price has been paid and the bones are therefore not returnable, they are given a slave's burial on the river bank near her husband's village.

Of utmost importance for the relations between the living and the dead is their sex. But what is the sex of the dead? Alternative historians never tire of pointing out that the historical dead – the famous of memorials and history books – are almost all dead white males. In many parts of the world, as women become socially important, they are increasingly classified as symbolic males. So in Benin a Queen Mother who has become a paragon of female success and fertility is treated and buried as a man.

If there is no flesh, therefore no sex, there can still be gender. Hence in much of China, women were traditionally believed to be plunged after death into a pond of gore in punishment for the polluted blood shed in childbirth in this world.

Among the Shona of Zimbabwe-Mozambique, ancestorhood centres on the idea of male potency. Pre-pubescent boys cannot become ancestors nor can old men who become impotent, no matter how many their children. Nor, of course, can most women (those not re-classified as men). Ritual concern is with rain, so that to overcome a drought, girls execute obscene gestures and sing bawdy songs with 'brothers' to stimulate the ancestors to orgasmic downpour. This also relates to the belief that men contribute the bones, or ethereal element, to children, while women give flesh, the earthly part. After death, the two sexes have different destinations. Men go to the sky, women to the soil.*

The Tetum of Timor take an opposed view. This world is dominated by men, the world of ghosts by women. So although both male and female exist, whenever spirits appear, they are women.

In Africa, women say things like 'I lived in that village until I became a man.' What they are talking about is the menopause. It is not unusual, in traditional cultures, to run through a number of genders in the course of life – and death.

Basic ideas like dry and wet can be used to organize gender. In a Cameroonian village I once lived in, children are seen as largely androgynous until boys are 'dried' at circumcision and girls become 'wet' through menstruation. Thereafter ageing leads to increasing dryness until women cease to menstruate and become 'dry like men'. Since the dead impregnate women (they are reincarnated in new children), when forced to think about it, people accept that this means they are male but their thought does not naturally follow such lines.

Instead, the female dead are subjected to a rite of rich ambiguity. The focus is a woman's water jar. It is dressed as a boy about to be circumcised, and danced with but the paraphernalia attached to the jar include throwing-knives that are a sign of the rainchief's ability to control the wet and dry seasons. All agree that this is a sort of counterpart to the treatment of men's skulls after death by which they cease to be merely dead and become ancestors. An

*Jacobson-Widding, 1990

outsider can fit the ritual readily into a pattern whereby the wet-
ness of women is regulated at different stages of their lives as they
become more or less strongly marked as female, but this is the
interpretation of anthropologists, not the informants. Assumptions
only become articulated beliefs when confronted by an alien view
and some cultures have no experts paid to formulate them.

The point is perhaps that in much of the world it is not enough
just to die to become an ancestor, any more than merely ageing
makes you an adult. Active ritual transformation is required and
for that you depend on the living. In most cultures not to marry
and have children therefore condemns you to an eternal immatu-
rity. Without descendants to respect and feed you, you quickly
cease to exist. The LoDagaa of Ghana tuck the penis of a dead
bachelor shamefully under his waistbelt in the way it is worn by a
little boy and his bow will not be placed on the ancestral shrine for
his descendants because they do not exist. It will be broken and
tossed away as a thing of no consequence. So to 'live on in one's
children' is not a poetic image or a nod towards the eternity of
DNA as in the West. It is a remark about sustenance, for the dead
must be fed by, and in turn look after, the living.

The Baule of Ivory Coast see the relations between this world and
the spirit realm (*blolo*) as more regular and balanced. *Blolo* is the
place from which we come and to which we return on death. It is
a more perfect, happier version of this world, a place of great
indulgence. Those who return from comatose states are incoher-
ent because they are still drunk with the copious palm wine that
flows on the other side. Balance implies that many births into this
world will be followed by many deaths to restore equality in the
other.

A troubled adolescence, or marital problems involving sterility
or impotence, alert a human that he or she has a spouse on the
other side who is discontented. The clincher is erotic dreams
involving someone of the other sex they have never seen before.

It can be solved by commissioning a wooden sculpture that
makes visible and controllable the unseen lover with whom the

owner then goes through a sort of marriage ceremony. The duties offered are many and various, from feasts to lustrations with oil and kaolin. Thursday nights, however, are reserved for the sexual enjoyment of the spirit partner, the earthly spouse being ejected.

The statues exemplify the Baule notion of male and female beauty, with their regular features, fine musculature and long, elegant necks. Whereas formerly they showed elders with beards and women with elaborate bodily scarification, the statues have kept up with changing tastes. Nowadays they may well show a woman in a chic trouser suit and a pouting cool dude in high-fashion Western dress and sunglasses.

———◈———

'You did not know the dead, but you will want to come and say hello to the family.' I was wandering through the back streets of Jakarta and bumped into a group of men carrying the corpse to the cemetery. A man at one end was having a desperate time trying to carry a metal-shafted umbrella over the deceased's head without hitting the live electric wires. I shook some hands in the most respectful way I knew and inquired whisperingly whether he had been married or had children.

'Not yet,' they murmured with downcast eyes.

Indonesian, in common with many South-East Asian languages, has a number of words for 'no' and 'not'. Their use constitutes a subtly coercive view of the essential nature of life. To the question of whether one is married, there are only two possible replies, 'Yes' or 'Not yet'. A simple 'No' is impossible since life – and death – without marriage is unthinkable.

There is no reason why the dead cannot marry even with the living. The Nuer of the Sudan arrange for a man to beget offspring in the name of a childless kinsman who has died. Since he may well not be able to afford another wife for the begetting of his own children, the upshot is that *he* in turn may remain childless.

'Ghost marriage' has to be practised on his behalf too. Several generations are then out of step, passing on the baton of parenthood.

Singapore Chinese sometimes pair off two unmarried dead so that their younger siblings may be free to wed without breaking the rule that older children must marry first. Similarly, in Taiwan, death does not bring an end to hopes of female matrimony since a new marriage is possible between the living and the dead. Domestic misfortune in a house may be attributed to the discontent of a young girl who has died unwed. Her family decide to find her a husband, usually a poor man, already married but attracted by the dowry. The dowry is made over to his living wife and the marriage is consummated with the spirit on the wedding night. Since the spirit is pure undiluted *yin*, the female principle, the man will be driven to a sexual frenzy, exhausted by multiple orgasms with the ghost and totally debauched. But this is for one day only. The next day the spirit becomes incorporated into the body of ancestors and never tastes again the joys of the flesh.

The African-influenced religions of Bahia, Brazil, allow practitioners to be possessed by gods. Their bodies may be borrowed not just for dancing but so that the deity may enjoy drinking and boisterous sexual intercourse. It seems that no firm line is drawn between the gods and the dead so that the latter too may not have to say a permanent farewell to the world of the senses thanks to the 'sacrifices' of worshippers.

Outside the major world religions, there is little concern with judgement and punishment in the next world for behaviour in this. Indeed, in Africa it is often the dead who judge the living and punish them in this life. The balance of power between the living and the dead is everywhere different. But if the dead go to another world, they must be prevented from returning except via proper channels. Much of traditional African political structure is based upon this. The elders are the normal channel through which the blessings of the dead may flow to the living. It is, however, taking matters too far to suggest that this is part of a quasi-universal transformation of death into life by which (male) fertility is distinguished from (female) sexuality and vested in men.* While the African dead ultimately do control the fertility of the living, the animals and the fields, this is often only in a negative way through their power of disruption. They are more likely to be responsible for sterility and disease, famine and drought, indeed death itself. These are simply the means by which they control their real concern, the basic relationships of social life.

This power is established retrospectively. You fail to give an offering you owe them, commit incest with a woman too close in kinship and you may get away with it. Suddenly, years later, they pay you back with leprosy, a deformed child, or a dead cow. The dead are above all capricious, which makes them of great explanatory power. They fill in gaps in the process by which the world is made logical.

A refreshing article by Igor Kopytoff suggests that Westerners have badly misunderstood the whole notion of African 'ancestors' and the links between 'cosmology' and 'social structure'.† He notes that among the Suku of Zaire the main distinction is between those who are senior and those who are junior, whether they be alive or dead. There is not even a word for 'ancestor'. The dead remain active members of the clan and act within the same legal framework as the living. They have the same powers to confer or refuse blessings and hence fertility. They can be contacted on clan business by elders who act as middlemen and from this it follows that relations with the dead are seen as following clan lines. So what is stressed is not notions of the next world but the powers of the dead in this. These powers, in turn, are simply those of eldership exercised by the living. There is no need to speak of 'projecting social structure onto cosmology.' The living and the dead are *both* members of the group. Nor is this phenomenon limited to Africa. Mark Hobart has pointed out that accounts of contemporary Balinese economic behaviour are hopelessly in-

*Bloch, 1982
†Kopytoff, 1971

92

adequate unless the calculations include the dead and those yet unborn as active members of the community.*

All this may be more relevant to ourselves than we realize. The loss of identity and purpose suffered by the retired in the West is probably due to their having spent their lives struggling up in hierarchies of power from which they are suddenly cast adrift. In Africa such hierarchies continue through respected elderhood and beyond the grave.

A very successful nineteenth-century notion was 'life-force', the idea that a person had a finite amount of vital energy that would slowly be spent through life until it ran out, at which point death would ensue. It seemed to explain a number of phenomena, the boisterousness of the young, the slow movements of the old, the analogy of death with sleep. It justified a certain cost-effective way of life, Protestant thrift, in the expenditure of energy, encouraged the idea that male orgasm was weakening, and cultivated a semi-invalid engagement with the world. In the late twentieth century we have replaced this idea with its opposite, the philosophy of 'use it or lose it', activity as an unlimited good, exercise as life-promoting. Now it is time itself, the individual lifespan, that is the scarce good.

The Anglo-Saxons saw the whole world not as progressing but as running downhill. 'Every day this mortal world declines and fades away,' wrote the poet. The end of the world was in sight. So people no longer lived as long as Methuselah and the monuments of the Roman empire – believed to have been built by giants – were now beyond the skills of the living.

In much of the world, issues of life and death are still seen as our forefathers saw them, a matter of a limited good or a world on the

*Hobart, 1994

wane and often this imposes an interchange of energy with out-siders or the dead. Nowadays, 'life force' seems a hopelessly vague and mystical notion similar to the 'cosmic energy' of New Agers. It is another phlogiston-like idea that adds nothing but is used to paper over the cracks of thought by the invention of an unidenti-fiable substance.

Yet anthropology is full of similar ideas. *Mana, wakan, orenda, ase* – such notions stalk the pages of ethnography, often invoked as explanatory principles in the realm of death but not really understood. The New Guinean Hua people have a concept of 'vital essence' called *nu*.* It occurs in the form of sexual fluids, faeces, urine, breath, body odour, saliva, hair, fingernails, blood, sap and fat. Anything that can be eaten is a source of *nu*. Sex involves the passing of *nu*. Children drain their parents of *nu* and so push them towards death. There is a fixed amount of it in the world so that its flow must be regulated. Marriage is tightly controlled. A stunted boy has to drink blood from his 'father' and at death, sons have to eat the corpse of their father and girls that of their mother. Should they fail to do so their crops, children and animals will not grow. Cannibalism is a way in which *nu* is transferred from one generation to the next.

But *nu* reflects the relationship between giver and receiver. So *nu* from some sources is polluting not strengthening. At its most ambivalent, it is associated with death and rotting, menstrual blood and the decay that lies within the composting bodies of women, the ultimate source of all *nu*. Men give their *nu* in the form of blood, animal flesh and garden plants to juniors but the flow cannot be reversed from young to old. Moreover, it seems that everywhere *nu* is leaking from the system so that men do not live as long as they did and even go bald earlier. This is not a world of limited good but of decreasing good like that of the Anglo-Saxons. Cannibalism is essential to prevent further *nu* loss and the running down of the whole world. *Nu* is a substance of infinite

*Sanday, 1986

elasticity moulded to justify the cultural world as natural and formed in the idiom of communication and exchange.

This language of the flow of mystical matter and energy between living and dead is not unlike the 'scientific', electrical idiom opposing life and death propounded by Sir James Murray in 1848 in his arguments against urban cemeteries. The decomposition of human remains, he assured the world roundly, caused terrible galvanic derangements so that vast pools of negative electricity were formed in graveyards, seeped into the soil and air and sucked away positive electricity from the living with potentially fatal consequences.

Other New Guinea peoples deal more directly in a language of body fluids, so that a sort of economy of life among the living results, a man being drained above all by demands on his supply of semen. The Marind traditionally held semen to be essential for growing boys and maintained that it increased health, cured wounds, improved weapons and eyesight and made plants grow. The female milk given to male babies must be replaced with male semen to develop boys so youths would be inseminated by their mother's brother. At some point, the flow would be reversed so that among the Etoro a boy would be inseminated by his sister's husband or betrothed.* Upon his marriage, however, he would then switch over from receiving semen to giving it to his wife's brother, who would similarly switch on marriage from receiving to giving. In societies where 'We marry the people we fight with' the flow of life depends on pumping semen around the system and topping up what you lose by sex with the enemy.

An alternative may be a form of plunder that involves death. The South American Jivaro know there to be a fixed number of possible individual identities in the world. Identities may be lost to the dead who lure away the unsuspecting to become their pets. They may be gained by a ritual of great complexity in which the heads of adult outsider Jivaro are taken, shrunk, disguised and

*Kelly, 1976

reprocessed to give a new identity to the group – just like a forged blank identity card.*

You see these shrunken heads in museums, eyes and mouths sewn shut, noses deformed to sneering snouts, long black rock-singer's hair, often martyrs to post-mortem dandruff. Sometimes, fakes are made from monkey heads to fool the unwary purchaser eager for foreign horrors. Yet the Jivaro themselves draw a firm line between the hunting of men and of animals. Nowadays, they have abandoned spears for rifles but any weapon that has killed a man immediately becomes disqualified for hunting animals. It must be traded away to foolish outsiders who know no better and confuse different kinds of death.

Certain peoples such as the New Guinea Avatip or the Amerindian Desana do seem to have something like the Western notion of mass energy so that a headhunter's 'spirit' is augmented by that of his victims in the sort of arithmetical fashion that would be comprehensible to an accountant.†

Yet even here names and identity are involved too, in the inter-action of living and dead, for names are often more than a label *for* the person, they are rather a part *of* it. The chief motive for head-hunting among the Marind-Anim of New Guinea was the short-age of names. Each child should receive the name of a headhunter's victim.‡ Asmat boys took the energy as well as the names of victims and used it for growth.** Should such a boy meet relatives of the deceased, these would accept him as their kinsman's replacement so that instead of exacting vengeance they would dance and sing for him and even give him presents.

Students of death abroad have largely defined the 'problems' raised by other cultures in terms of the way we confront death amongst ourselves. At a conference, I once met a Japanese anthropologist who, unbeknownst to either of us, had worked next door to me

*Descola, 1994
†Harrison, 1993:122
‡van Baal, 1966
**Zegwaard, 1968

in Africa. Like his prose he was very trim and precise but it took some time before I recognized in him the 'Frenchman' of whom the people there had spoken. We had a long and interesting chat about circumcision and its varieties and then moved on to 'religion'.

'I had intended to study their religion,' he said, 'but it was just not interesting, so I looked at economics instead. Their system for pricing yams and its interaction with city markets was most fascinating.'

Religion not interesting? Didn't they have a rather complicated form of ancestor worship involvng bones and the destruction of the skull and all sorts of exchanges between the dead and the living?

'Yes, yes. As I said, not interesting.'

He was, of course, a Buddhist who had a shrine to his departed parents in his living room, on which regular offerings were made. Later he let drop that he had taken to Africa some bone from his dead father's leg, carefully wrapped in white cloth, to ensure protection during his fieldwork. For me, ancestor worship was something to be described and analysed. For him, it would be the *absence* of such links between the living and the dead that would require special explanation.

5

Only Flesh and Blood

'There are three unions in this world, Christ and the Church,
husband and wife, spirit and flesh.'

Saint Augustine (AD 354–430)

Lindow Man resides on the first floor of the British Museum.
His more demotic alias is Pete Marsh, a name invented from the
place of his discovery in 1984. Since the unearthing – or unpeat-
ing – of the Danish Bog People by the appropriately named
Professor Glob, Britain had always aspired to its very own Ancient
Briton. Not that Pete is all that ancient, somewhere between 300
BC and AD 100. The Museum's information on him seeks a little
desperately to spice up his story. Stripped, clubbed, garotted,
exsanguinated and dumped in a bog, could he be the victim of an
early botched mugging, that of a beginner experimenting clumsily
with every possible means of homicide? Not so. Pete's demise,
claims the information panel, conjuring up a world entirely of its
own imagination, is 'evidence for a savage ritual.' We are even
told, by implication, who-dun-it. The presence of mistletoe
pollen points the finger at the Druids but we can't be too adamant.
After all, they might sue.

Cleaned, freeze-dried, irradiated, CAT-scanned, intestines and
brain cavity forensically probed, Lindow Man lies on a bed of peat
in subdued light, arms curled as if to rock a baby. A hologram,
viewed through glass, offers his face swimming in and out of focus
as in a green goldfish bowl and invites physiognomic speculation.

The reality of the body is like a cartoon character, flattened by a steamroller but curiously intact, and a 'reconstructed' artist's impression nearby has turned his face into that of an earnest sixties folksinger. Only the Japanese are sufficiently post-modern to photograph the hologram rather than the corpse itself. The skin over the skull has shrunk down to a version of that most versatile of English headgear, the flat cap, simultaneously the mark of sporting members of the upper classes and shiftworkers awaiting redundancy notices. There is, of course, no possibility of mistaking one for the other. Here, the shrunken face exhibits unshaven bristle, so on him the cap is the stamp of proletarian Pete, the dosser, not dignified Lindow Man.

But the information panel will not have it. There is evidence of manicure, an absence of the wear and tear of agricultural labour, even fox fur accessories. Pete is a toff. Safely tucked away in the accompanying publication is a reminder that Tacitus mentioned bog burial as the punishment for *le vice anglais* – or *germanique* as it would have been then. This is passed over in silence.

Pete is constantly surrounded by people, whispering, nudging, posing. Why do they come? It seems he has something for everyone, is relevant to the present, part of the function of the museum as time machine. A French tour guide is there, spouting omniscient trivia. She points. 'The oldest *Anglais*.' So Pete is English now? But the place hadn't been invented then. It's like giving Asterix an EU passport. 'A Celt,' says a man to his son in confident Glaswegian tones. 'The hair is red like your own.' Yes but *all* interred hair turns red. Down the hall there's a predynastic Egyptian known as Ginger. 'Very *brown*,' says a Home Counties lady doubtfully as if blackballing his application for membership of the golf club. 'So,' concludes a small, comforted Japanese to his friend, 'in those days *all* people short.'

The fascination seems to lie in the flesh. If Pete were a skeleton, he'd be just dead matter, changing from a person to stuff. With flesh still on, he's an individual, someone with an identity and a nationality. He's got a *face*. In fact, now he's got three.

The Church of England does not allow funerals without a body. Perhaps this goes some way to explain the British obsession with recovering bodies after a disaster. Yet while many other peoples see ritual as necessary for the progress of the dead to another state, Western researchers have stressed its necessity as part of a grieving process through which the *living* are provided with a series of clear stages that lead back to full life. This allows therapists to justify the awfulness of funerals within a more general framework, since a common Western model of addiction and mental disorder requires the sufferer to 'touch bottom' before he can begin to rise again and truly be cured.

The components of the physical body may be many and numerous. Commonly a line is drawn between flesh/blood and bone, the corruptible and the relatively clean and permanent. As Levi-Strauss first pointed out, this often ties up with kinship, each side of a marriage seen as contributing one of the essential components to the children so that it is impossible to understand death without looking at theories of conception.[*] The flesh/bone distinction may often be seen as the whole physical basis of kinship, as the mixing of 'blood' once was with us. In many cultures, marriage is best understood as simply part of a continuous series of exchanges between groups and contributions towards new persons are part of this exchange. Once this is accepted, a whole series of speculations are thrown open to the anthropologist at play.

A common Asian model is that the father's semen produces the bones of a child, the mother's blood its flesh. The same line between flesh and bone occurs among the Shona of the Zimbabwe-Mozambique border. When they divide up animal flesh, they say, 'The rib is for the daughter of the father. The meat is for the mother. Because the father is the one who gives the bone to the child, while the mother gives the meat.'[†]

[*]Levi-Strauss, 1969:373
[†]Jacobson-Widding, 1991:61

Since Westerners define themselves as individuals by asserting ownership over their own bodies, the opposite of a freehold individual is a slave. On marriage, we have severe problems even with assigning rights in our sexual parts. Other cultures may freely assign ownership of entire body components to others. The Rotinese of Eastern Indonesia (like the Mae-Enga of New Guinea) hold that the blood of an individual legally belongs to the mother's brother. If anyone sheds even his own blood through accidental injury he must pay compensation to the mother's brother. The mother's brother also receives payments of compensation on his sister's sons's death since this is primarily an offence against *him*.

It is planned to send the remains of 20,000 noses back from Japan to Korea. The noses were sliced off by Japanese Samurai as war trophies during the 1597 Japanese invasion and are now to be buried, nearly four hundred years later, on a battlefield near the southern port city of Puan as a gesture of reconciliation.

We forget that the boundaries of our bodies are a matter of convention. In Java, the stress is less on the destruction of the body at death than on its reassembly. Traditionally, persons of rank never discard hair, nail clippings or teeth. They are carefully preserved, in a place safe from witches, and buried with the corpse. After all, they too are part of the body and belong together.

There is a Malagasy story that explains the different ingredients of a person:

> In the beginning two gods created man. The earth god formed him of wood or clay, the god of heaven gave life. But the creators disagreed among themselves, and therefore each was to take his own again. It is for this reason that men die, which implies that life goes back to heaven, whereas the body is returned to the earth.*

*Abrahamsson, 1951:115

101

—◦◦◦—

Death frequently involves division. There is the property of the deceased. Inheritance may pass differently according to sex. Among the Minang of Sumatra, land and houses pass from mother to daughter though moveable goods pass through men. 'Men,' say Minang women, blowing at their fingertips, 'are like dust.'

Among the Iriama of Tanzania the house may be physically dismantled, and the parts associated variously with livestock and grain returned to different sides of the family. Elsewhere, the corpse itself is divided up. In some cases the blood goes to the mother's kin, the bone to the father's.

The Melanesian Trobrianders have a slightly different system. They are famous within anthropology* for the belief that men play no part in the impregnation of women and that a child's father is merely its relative through marriage. The publication of this claim triggered a considerable storm in the teacup of anthropology that continues to the present day. Further research has only slightly modified the view that a child takes all its substance from the mother, the father simply shaping the foetus in the womb and affecting its form. The crucial factor in pregnancy is the entrance into a woman of a spirit of her clan group that is then incarnated in maternal blood to form the child. This fits neatly with the way Trobrianders trace descent and the transmission of rights through women rather than men, constituting groups through the female line. The word *dala*, 'blood', also means the sub-clan to which a person belongs. While the husband's semen does not actually become part of the substance of the child it controls its appearance, so the opposition made here is not that between flesh and bone but rather between substance and form.

Even after birth, the father's side is heavily implicated with

*Malinowski, 1916 and 1929

shaping the child. He massages its head into beautiful contours while only his sister can perform the beauty magic that makes the maturing young physically attractive.

This distinction between substance and form is crucial after death, for the exchanges that occur between groups then are best seen not as 'reaffirming endangered social relations' – according to conventional clichés about the meaning of funerals – but as 'de-conceiving' the deceased.* The tracing of actual exchanges is a matter of fiendish complexity but, broadly, women give gifts to regain ancestral property (blood, identity, personal names, coconut and betel palms, decorations and rights to land) that have passed out through the deceased. The groups that make up society, whose elements are mixed in any individual, are unscrambled again by women who embody the enduring substance of the group. The hut in which a man kept his yams, the focus of social exchanges between men, is demolished.

A dead person's body may not be handled by his or her own group, who may not show grief, but only by relatives through marriage – which here include a man's sons. The flesh of the dead man would be lethal to his own 'blood' so they pay others to deal with it.

The sons have the important job of sucking the putrefaction from the bones of his exhumed corpse and washing them of rotting flesh in the sea so that his spirit can travel back across the water and ultimately be reincarnated. This disagreeable job is explained by Trobrianders as repaying the care the father showed in feeding his sons mashed yam and cleaning away faeces and urine when they were babies. They are dismantling him, the way he constructed them and converting him into dry bone as he made them into hard men. The bones of the corpse are then shared out among those linked to the deceased through marriage – again not 'blood' – and may be made into ornaments to be worn, together with his hair, nails and personal possessions. A man's skull may be converted into a lime-pot for his widow and his long bones into

*Mosko, 1985

lime spatulas to be licked when chewing betel nut. The white lime, when mixed with betel nut, gives bright red clotted juice in a manner echoing Trobriand notions of conception. The jawbone often becomes a necklace, recalling the way fathers give necklaces and earrings to their children. The bones will be passed around from one relative to another over the years, be decorated and change their form constantly. Finally, their permanent substance will be handed back to his own people who ritually sever those links established between the deceased and other groups. So the body, the spirit, the survivors, all experience a similar process of gradual disintegration, separation and circuitous return to origins.

Yet it would be wrong to see the role of women as exclusively positive. Among the wives that give material to create children lurk some who infect their young with witchcraft. They come out at night and feast on the flesh of their victims – especially those of their own 'blood'.* Here is the negative side of women's powers of transformation, the negative power of blood and biology, an inversion of the sucking off the bones of putrefied flesh performed by the sons to release their father's spirit.

———⟨⟨⟨⟨⟩⟩⟩⟩———

Penang in the rain failed to deliver the romance of the tourist brochures, and the bus station, a huge, stained concrete monstrosity, was not looking its limited best in the downpour. The men on the tea stall were doing their utmost to be cheerful, pouring scalding tea in great milky twists from one jug to another at arm's length, clearly showing off. Suddenly an umbrella prodded me.

'You!' she said. I turned to see a Chinese nun, wimpled and habited under a long mac and Edna Everidge glasses. 'It's you, isn'i?' It was hard to deny it, but she looked very angry.

*Tambiah, 1983

104

'Er . . . me?'

'I saw you on television last night, isn'i',' she accused.

'It's possible.' Ambushed with an Egyptian mummy by a local film crew, I had done an interview to promote an exhibition of grave goods, on loan from Britain, at the National Museum. I had been cajoled and prodded into stumbling through a few answers in broken Malay. Perhaps it had gone out last night.

'Ha! I thought so. Well we Chinese don' like death you know and you come on and show dead body all wrapped up from Egypt and dead man's clothe. All sticky. Filthy thing. What for you bring Muslim nonsense like that?'

'Well, strictly speaking, of course, the Egyptians weren't Muslim.' Lead her off into side issues, I thought.

She snorted, 'That not a real body with flesh not just bone. Can't be. Only Christian saint don't go bad.'

I had had this conversation before. It was at a Christian Indonesian village where two Muslim schoolteachers took the line that God preserved the bodies of Muslim saints to show their virtue but Christian bodies only as examples of wickedness to the faithful.

'My sister's little boy so frighten, he cry all night.'

'Well, I'm very sorry. Perhaps if you brought him to the exhibition, it would show him there's nothing to be frightened of.'

'I took him. He scream a house down. Also is catchcombs.'

'Catchcombs?'

'Yes,' she raised her umbrella as if to strike and fired off instead another semantic scattergun. 'Catchcombs, bones under Rome, early Christian.'

'Ah, catacombs.' The exhibition did, in fact, include a sort of evocation of the Christian catacombs, with glowing fake bones arranged in patterns in the dark.

'Catchcombs very black. The girls go in there so they can be afraid, scream at the bones and grab the boys. It's disgusting in cemetery. Sins of *flesh* don' belong with bones.' This was actually pretty accurate. A lot of tousled young people *were* in there, happily giving and receiving fleshly comfort.

'I come back next week. Maybe I just stay in catchcombs all day and shine my torch in their silly face.'

———◦◦◦———

In medieval Europe it was not uncommon to leave money to have one's body dismembered. In 1284, a certain Chevalier Jacques d'Anniviers, asked that his flesh and bones should be separated and sent to different monastic foundations. Chevalier Jacques was multiplying the number of sacred employees working for the salvation of his soul. After death, there was still a great deal of divine work to be done to secure the release of the soul from purgatory or to arrange intercession on its part by saints.

From papal denuciations of the practice, such as that of Boniface VIII in 1299, we know that it was common to transport the dead around Europe to the monastery of their choice. To overcome the problem of physical decay, the intestines would be removed and buried and the rest of the cadaver occasionally cooked to free the bones which were then marinaded in perfumed wine and pepper. When Queen Mary claimed that they would find the world 'Calais' engraved on her heart when she died, she spoke as one who expected her organs to be viewed after the 'ripping of the corpse'. Hearts might often find a separate place of interment, like those of the French royal house at St Denis.

Embalming, it seems, overlapped with 'pickling' and drew on techniques for the dressing of carcasses and the preservation of flesh for human consumption – necessary in the days when most animals had to be slaughtered before winter. These techniques hover uncertainly between excessive regard for the flesh and contempt for it. Pope Boniface chose to see it as the latter. 'An abuse of abominable savagery, practised by some of the faithful in a horrible way and inconsiderately.'

Where bodies are buried twice or otherwise undergo secondary treatment, the reduction of flesh to bone provides a natural timetable for the separation of spirit from body and the living from the dead just as the lingering of Walt Disney's cadaver in a California freezer is a denial that his time is over. It is one of the semi-constants of death that it is only (wet) rotting flesh that is polluting while (dry) bones are relatively clean and will be handled with equanimity.

Another curiosity is that while flesh is temporary, tattoos are often classed as permanent, having a memorial quality. The Ekoi of southern Nigeria embossed their arms with circular, coin-like scarifications known as 'ghost food'. The ghost of the dead would be able to use them as money to buy sustenance.

Gujaratis and the Newar of Nepal hold that those without tattoos will not be allowed into Heaven, a fact that possibly derives from their use as marks of maturity.* Torajans still say that the young should be burnt on the forearms to ensure they have light to see by in the dark and upside-down world of the dead.

The sexes may be seen as differently implicated in the whole physical biology of death. Maurice Bloch has argued that many cultures encumber women with the responsibility for biological creation and so individual death.[†] Often it is women who are obliged to associate themselves with the worst of pollutions, intimate association with the corpse and its putrefaction. The phenomenon, however, is more general. Even in Victorian England a woman might be plunged into deepest mourning for one of her husband's relatives while he remained relatively unencumbered. As the *Woman's World* of 1889 pointed out, men 'mourn by proxy.' The segregated, decorated and impractical Victorian wife was above all a marker of her husband's social, moral and spiritual status, a social litmus paper that showed *his* ritual condition.

Moreover, the normal scheme can be reversed. Among the matrilineal Khasi of India, people are held to be composed of bone from the mother, while the soft, fleshy parts come from the

*Rubin, 1988:139, 198
[†]Bloch, 1982

father.* So in the initial, polluting, fleshy stages of death, it is primarily men who handle the corrupt body and pass the clean bone to women.

Such ideas are too frequently dismissed by Western researchers as mere political metaphor. Yet the idea that the individual is a 'portfolio' of elements and shares common substance with certain others justifies beliefs as diverse as the 'naturalness' of kinship and magical communication at a distance. What is individual from one perspective, for example physical appearance, may be seen as deeply communal from another, in the form of 'looking like' or 'taking after.' What we see as merely social identity is elsewhere seen as physical and material.

There is no need for the sexes to agree on a common view of the role of each in procreation and death. It has been suggested that in Chinese society there is a traditional female view that differs strongly from that of men.[†] For while men stress the clean, male purity of bone that passes down the lineage and the dangers of pollution, women home in on the cyclicity of life and death. Each specializes in the two extremes of ritual activity. Men as 'splitters', resisting change and maintaining boundaries, women are 'lumpers' mixing contraries. So women sing dirges not just at funerals but also at weddings, when they socially 'die' for their own lineage. And daughters-in-law absorb fertility from the dead by freeing their hair to rub it against the coffin of the deceased and even convert cloths of mourning to make handy baby-carriers.

In Southern China, the dead undergo secondary burial. After some time in the earth, the bones are removed and cleaned of any remaining flesh. They are then reassembled in the foetal position, placed in a ceramic vessel, a 'golden womb', and allocated to a tomb whose form has more than a passing similarity to the female genitals, with its large curved opening barred by an erect ancestral tablet.[‡] One of the most terrible things that can be done to a tomb

*Arhem, 1988
[†]Martin, 1988
[‡]Thompson, 1988:104

is to smear it with the blood of a black dog – equated with dead menstrual blood – so that the benevolent influence and fertility that flows from the pure male ancestors is cut off.

———❦———

It was a day fit for a funeral, one of those bitter winter days where it never quite gets light, where everything is grey and undefined. Greasy drizzle seeped from a sky that contained the only point of colour, a red smear of sunlight like a sore eye.

The car pulled up on dank tarmac and we got out into a wind that stung our faces. Other doors of other cars clunked and thudded behind us without echo. There was none of the slickly colour-coordinated black of society mourning. Notions of funeral dress seemed at an awkward stage: the complete black ensemble would appear affected, but not to make a token effort would be sloppy. Even the old, for whom such events must have been a regular thing, were oddly-equipped. One man seemed on the verge of personally reinventing those traditions where you mark mourning by wearing your clothes inside out or putting your knickers on your head. Mostly there were darkish suits and ties but overcoats were of bold, bright colours that year – especially the women's. Formality overriding all other conventions, the women had generally pressed bright wedding hats back into service and tricked them out with a black ribbon or other black decoration. One wore an incongruous black veil on a bird's nest of crimson petals. We looked like a group of refugees.

Even the unwilling had tears in their eyes from the chill. We shuffled in, clutching damp hankies, snuffling from cold, grief, social convention. My father's coffin was already there, a person reduced to an item of Edwardian furniture, draped in weedy-looking flowers. On these occasions the mind slides off into incidentals. Where do they get flowers in mid-winter? The wreaths were packed with too much leaf, looking like the holly creations the aspiring middle-class were being persuaded to hang on their front doors at Christmas's approach.

The crematorium was a rational municipal building designed for measured grief, built in a raised brick herringbone pattern that crumbles to dust with time. On a journey through English life you meet many such buildings – places dispensing municipal practicalities without feeling. At the back was the chimney, embarrassingly Auschwitz-like. We looked at it in terror of seeing a gaffe of black smoke.

There were big, clear windows to let in rational light but today there was no light. Inside was what they like to call a worship-space suitable for conversion to a basketball court in the evenings. Some sort of heating hissed hot air – smelling like the searing pipes of my infant school behind which we deliberately dropped wax crayons in our first acts of vandalism. We all sniffed, excessively sensitive to fugitive smells of burning. It is one of the marks of ritual that everything becomes potentially significant, meaning more than itself, making the invisible visible.

My father had always been radically anti-clerical, much given at Christmas to comic impersonations of prating parsons but in his last years he had joined some sort of spiritualist church and claimed supernatural communication. There had been 'messages from the other side': about the bitter winter to come, the sudden death of an aunt, subsequently confirmed, but these had all been too often retold, smoothed and recalibrated to fit in with what we now knew. We no longer recalled what had really happened. We remembered only that we remembered, like children told by their parents what their earliest memories are.

When they first diagnosed the kidney failure and told him his days were numbered, he had said simply, 'Oh bugger!' Just that. In tones of mild annoyance; I had admired that. Then he had 'organized things', insisting on moving, absurdly, to an area where he knew no one, to a house too small with a garden too large, making things worse. My mother, always squeamish over blood, had been chained to a regimen of dialysis, pushing needles into squirming arteries, pumping gore through serpentine tubes snaking around her head.

At the end my father made my mother promise that the next time he had a heart attack she would call no one but just let him die. Twice already they had smugly brought him back from death to a life he no longer wanted; they would turn away embarrassed when he said he wanted an end to it all. Now he was gone but his absence was so acute it was almost a tangible presence. The spiritualists could smell that in the air.

There was no parson, which was just as well. Instead, one of the leading lights of the spiritualist church, in black suit and tie, would 'witness'. His model was a press conference. He was sweating, used notes, stumbled once or twice over my father's name. Had he ever known him? Certainly the character portrait, with its list of smug virtues, didn't sound familiar. The edifying content was *Reader's Digest* thoughts on mortality and eternity not so different after all from what a prating parson would have given us. A constant theme was that Man was more than mere flesh and blood. Death was where the cleanly spiritual triumphed over soiled flesh, a sort of disposable nappy. It had now been flung away and the spirit was free. I felt angry at the hypocrisy of it all. We were colluding in a dishonourable pretence and we knew it. Rude reality was showing through the holes in the ritual.

The dull emptiness in your stomach is called grief. But grief isn't the right word. It's a sort of cocktail of acrid emotional pollutants of which the strongest element is surely guilt. Guilt for sins of omission and commission or perhaps simply because when there is an emotional vacuum, nameless guilt just floods in to fill it up. Part of what we feel for our loved ones is a sort of addict's dependence. Presence may not bring ecstasy but absence is unbearable. Because we tidy death away from all but those most closely affected, it was a long time since I had been to an English funeral.

Death in the family had been tamed to a series of anecdotes. There was one about my mother during the war, having to break the news to a woman that her husband had been killed by a bomb as he cycled to work. Her response had become part of family folklore. 'Oh God, no,' she had gasped weakly, 'now everyone will know he was wearing one of my vests.'

I think there were hymns, but not the comfortingly meaningless hymns from school that carried feelings of nostalgia. In these, although the tunes were familiar the words were wrong, all too spiritually correct and involving no allusion to a transcendental higher God. I had an intensely irritated feeling of being interfered with.

You could see on the faces of the spiritualists that they were looking forward to tuning in at the next meeting, scratching at the crystal of death with their 'cats whiskers'. My father was a potential new transmitter of information about 'over there'. If this were Africa I'd be interested in what they thought. It would be placed in inverted commas, immune from scepticism. 'The Bongo-Bongo,' I would write with easy confidence, 'believe that . . .'

A trapdoor opened as in pantomine and the coffin disappeared, but in no puff of smoke. A priest I talked to once told me how significant the door was. Something was required that opened and shut, it signalled an ending, the mark that it was all over. The front row of people leaned forward, perhaps hoping for a whiff of flame. I couldn't wait to get away.

At the house was an embarrassingly small group of largely unfamilar relatives, a parody of kinship, testament to the failure of the Western family. The symbolism of the cold meats was horribly obvious.

'Dreadful,' one said with clicking false teeth. 'When I were a lad there'd be horses with black plumes. What did we get this time? A bloody van. Not a hearse. A van like we were going to a building site. It's not right.'

Sherry circulated. 'How much did you have to pay, Kath?' asked the clicking teeth.

My mother told him unwillingly. Funerals, like gifts, should not speak their price. He hissed breath sharply over his teeth.

'Eeh. Not cheap. I know the price of gas has a gone up but still. . .'

In a few weeks' time he would send a Christmas card covered with tinselly snow crystals and picturing a rudimentary manger full of quizzically-faced beasts. 'Silent Nights' it would read.

6

Political Deaths

'Alas! I suppose I am turning into a god.'
Emperor Vespasian (*d*. AD 79)

There is a green hill far away without a city wall. The wall was
blown up by the British and the city is Malacca, once the largest
port in South-East Asia, now a sleepy town that seethes with racial
suspicion between the Chinese, the Malays, the Indians and the
'Portuguese'. As soon as the East India Company got hold of it in
the eighteenth century, they decided to demolish the town as an
encouragement to the people to move to their own rival settlement of Penang. It was saved by the intervention of Stamford
Raffles who pointed out the deep attachment of the citizens to
their native soil and water, especially since their ancestors were
buried here. They still are, on the hill that ripples with womb-
shaped Chinese tombs. Any tourist has to visit.

Yet, the first thing you see, silhouetted against the sky, are
youths in polychrome running gear compulsively loping round
and round, doing step-ups on the tombs, supporting themselves
on the memorial tablets as they stretch groin and thighs.

Americanization of the East, you think. Dreadful impiety. In a
minute they will jog away to eat a burger, take in a movie and
communicate about their relationships. But when you enquire
about the joggers with a man who sells incense at the gate, he is
suddenly enthusiastic. 'This is politics! They are our heroes! They

are sweating to protect our culture! The Malays want to demolish the cemetery to build flats. They have too many children, not like us. Where will our dead go? When we protested, they put our leaders in jail. If we try to march, they ban it. But no one can stop our boys running in our own graveyard. So every day, they show who it belongs to and the bodies they defend it with.'

The bodies of the great are as dangerously political as their owners were when alive. Lenin's death came as something of an embarrassment to the anti-ritual Soviet leadership since no one quite knew what to do with it. The solution was the miraculously rapid construction of his tomb (36 hours) in 1924 by an army of volunteer workers intoxicated by revolutionary fervour.* The preservation of the body solved the second problem of how to dispose of it. Henceforth, 'fraternal, socialist countries' were expected to have their leaders preserved as part of the communist package and Soviet experts have set their mark for eternity on Ho Chi Minh and, more recently, Kim Il Sung. Lenin, however, was the only dead leader ever allowed to retain a Communist Party membership card – number one – showing who was really still in charge of ideology. While the incorruptible body might be seen by the peasants as a continuation of the traditional veneration of saints' relics, the Soviet leadership seem to have urged its interpretation as an anti-mystical act, an engaging and debunking of the Church's claims of saintly preservation, neatly showing ritual's ability to transmit two totally opposed messages at the same time.

Preservation, or even monumentalisation, of the great, although it seems to defeat time, always allows history to express a change of opinion. The dismemberment and defilement of the tombs of denounced party members by Red Guards has encouraged most of the prominent Chinese dead since Mao to have their bodies cremated and the ashes dispersed. But even this may not be enough. In 1594, the Turks, to punish Serbian disloyalty, removed the sacred bones of Saint Sava from his tomb and publicly burnt

*Binns, 1979, 1980

115

them, scattering the ashes to the four winds. The spot at which this infamous act occurred has now itself become a place of pilgrimage, replacing the missing bones.

When the Americans pulled out of the Panama Canal Zone, they surreptitiously removed their dead lest they become hostages to a capricious political future. Equally, pictures of the remains of an American marine being dragged joyfully around Mogadishu, kicked and spat upon, did more to ensure the withdrawal of their forces from Somalia in 1993 than his actual death.

> I suddenly, impiously, remembered a joke making the rounds among particularly defiant Peking intellectuals in the summer of 1977. A *t'u-pao-tzu*, (bumpkin) from the countryside visits his city cousin, who takes him to see Mao's tomb. 'Ai-ya,' the bumpkin says. 'It's so big! Chairman Mao always wanted to be just like one of us. He never wanted to distance himself from the masses. How could you build him such a big and imposing *ling-mu* (mausoleum)?' 'Oh,' answers the city cousin, 'just to prove that he's really dead.'*

Funerals have a special place in political struggles. Using the paradox that is death, they convert defeat into triumph. The dead become martyrs, trophies of the cause, proof of its strength and in the heightened emotional atmosphere of the funeral, grief becomes converted into political enthusiasm. At Julius Caesar's funeral, Mark Antony interrupted his oration with bursts of formal lamentation shared by the crowd and a wax effigy lavishly illustrated with Caesar's twenty-three wounds was later exhibited to stir up feeling.

Not for nothing were IRA funerals more feared by British security forces than Republican marches and rallies. They were conducted in full military idiom, with men in uniform, a gun and

*Wakeman, 1988:256

a beret on the coffin, flags, firing in the air. Like in many rituals, IRA funerals would treat as given what were matters of high controversy i.e. that they were fighting a legitimate war, that there existed a separate and parallel IRA administration, that all were united in a common struggle about whose aims all were agreed. For police or army to interfere and contest those assertions was to molest the dead, to be vindictive, indecently to inject politics into what was a private show of grief.

Even the most individual of funerals can be generalized as supporting a cause or having a message. So-and-So's death can always be said to mark 'the end of an era'. In Britain this marks the distinction between the private and the public funeral. But any regular and repetitive proceeding attacks the uniqueness of the event so we are offended by the pre-packaged, impersonal nature of the hospital death and the plastic-wrapped warm-and-serve McRitual of burial itself.

The Murder Act of 1752 determined that the bodies of murderers were to be anatomically dissected, thus reinforcing the enduring connection in the English mind between respectability and 'decent' burial. In the early modern period, high treason was properly punished by the slicing away of the sex organs, disembowelling and burning of the intestines, hanging or beheading, dismemberment and exhibition of the body parts on city walls and gates. After the restoration of the British monarchy, the regicide, Oliver Cromwell, was disinterred from Westminster Abbey, hanged at the gallows and dismembered as if he were still a living traitor. This was not mere disrespect to a body. It was full legal process. At that time, after all, a corpse could still be arrested even for debt. Cromwell's critics at the moment of his death made much of his rapid decay but it is noteworthy that it still took eight blows to hack off the head. Hair was apparently still on the head when it was finally interred at Sidney Sussex College, Cambridge, in 1960.

The newspaper *Tchad et Culture* (October 1992), notes that the founding of political parties has disrupted funeral etiquette in

117

N'Djamena. Important burials are now mobbed by importuning politicians seeking to seduce votes from the bereaved. In the forlorn hope of attracting their support, they shower the mourners with money, lend them transport and go so far as to sit up tearfully two or three nights with the bodies of people they never even knew.

This is not unique. We assume too readily that a person's importance is directly reflected by the extravagance of their funeral or burial. Not so. The Berawan of Sarawak construct lavish tombs for the bones of total nonentities which are mere props for the ambitions of rising relatives.* It is the organizer who is celebrated and consolidated by the successful tomb on the river bank, not the hijacked tenant.

In the Middle Ages, physical decay of the corpse was a mark of general sin or – in women – lust. So the incorruption of the flesh of saints could be stressed and extended into a form of pseudo-life. St Cuthbert's tomb in Durham was repeatedly reopened to allow combing of the hair and cutting of the nails. In a curious dialogue, enemies of the Church have also tended to stress the fleshly envelope of the sacred and the absurdity of seeking to escape it. Thus both sides in religious debate home in on the slippery symbol of corruptible flesh. A Catholic commentator on the burial of Elizabeth I maintained that the onset of corruption had been so rapid that her coffin exploded.† During the Spanish Civil War, a special political detachment of the Republican forces was set up as a matter of priority to organize the disinterment and public exhibition of the rotted corpses of nuns in captured cities. In later times, the Peronists, using the same language to opposite effect, hijacked and exhibited the untainted corpse of Evita Peron on two continents.

In the Lower Congo, there was a rather unusual form of coffin called the *niombo*. The most striking version of this continued to

*Huntington and Metcalf, 1980
†Litten, 1992:42

be used by the Bwende people until the 1930s. The corpse of an important man or woman would first undergo prolonged smoking to dry it. Missionaries made much of the horrific scenes of the corpse being turned by the black-smeared wives over a slow fire inside the hut while they uttered piercing screams through the choking smoke, stench and swarms of bloated bluebottles. As much as a year later, when no further juices issued from the shrivelled cadaver, it was wrapped in mats and hundreds of cloths to create a huge bulbous figure up to three times the size of the original. The cloths would be donated by brothers-in-law and members of the deceased's own group. This monstrous effigy would then be painted bright red, decorated with the dead person's tattoos and a soft head wearing a chief's hat set atop the whole structure. The arms would be arranged in a dancer's pose. Amidst music, dancing and gunfire it would be buried in a huge excavation, standing up. Underneath it, several slaves might be pinned down in the tomb and buried alive.

Since eye-witness informants have long since disappeared, anthropologists have had a field day interpreting this ritual. In this area, cloth functioned as something of a cross between ration coupons and money, limiting access to wives, power and status. The 'earthing' of so much wealth, given by kin and supporters, could be seen as a powerful statement of individual and group achievement and loyalty. Important men would invest cash from trade in buying or fathering children on slaves who then joined the father's not the mother's group as would otherwise be the case. So the reduction of the real body and its replacement by a huge inflated simulacrum composed of 'cash' could be seen as representing a triumph of personal entrepreneurship over clan kinship – establishing that someone was simply 'made of money' rather than the stuff of the group.

The sculptures of ethnic art, so blithely called 'ancestor figures', even when they relate to the dead, have enormously varying relationships with the actual deceased. Some provide a physical object in which various sorts of spirit may take up permanent or temporary lodging. They can fill empty slots in the world left by death or eternalize an individual. Sometimes they cover the intellectual embarrassment of the death of someone, royal or divine, who is defined as more than mortal. An alternative is simply to deny the whole fact of royal death and mummify the body or otherwise erase it from memory.

In eastern Madagascar among the Antaisaka, the death of a ruler is concealed, burial happens at night and afterwards the deceased's name is changed. The Shilluk of the Sudan deal with the problem of royal succession by only having one king who is immortal. Nyikang, the culture hero, never dies. A candidate for the kingship fights a symbolic battle with the army of the wooden effigy of Nyikang, who defeats him and possesses his body. In a further confrontation over Nyikang's wife, it is the new king, embodying Nyikang, that is victorious. The effigy returns to its enclosure to await the next succession. The well-being of the whole kingdom is held to depend on the living king. Should he sicken or fail to satisfy his wives, according to tradition, he would be quietly murdered by being walled up alive. No body would ever be seen and the effigy of Nyikang would simply come out again to fill in.

⟞ɷɷ⟝

An island in Lake Toba sacred to the Batak of North Sumatra, Samosir has come down in the world. It was sucked into the hippy circuit in the 1960s, wrapped in aromatic cannabis smoke, until the government decided there was more money in selling romantic honeymoons to wealthy Singaporeans and cleaned it up. Many of the young people still speak an Americanized pop-pidgin where every sentence begins, 'Like, wow, man . . .'

120

It is impossible to escape the dancing doll, the *gale-gale*. They wheel it out all over the place for the tourists. It represents a young man in traditional dress with the scraped geometric face you see on ancient Indonesian sculpture. It waves, stoops and twists to accompanying music. From the back trail billowing sheets that conceal the operator, busy working the moving parts by pushing sticks and pulling strings. The whole thing is about as convincing as a green toupee.

The story goes that there was a king who had a son that he loved dearly. He was the most perfect youth that ever lived. Then he died and his father went nearly mad with grief. So they carved a statue that looked just like him. 'It looks like him,' said the king doubtfully, 'but he used to dance so beautifully. The statue does not dance.' So a clever man set it to dance for the king and he was happy before he died. Applause. Pass round the hat. Pose for photo with the effigy's arm round your shoulders.

Before the Toba Batak converted to Christianity, they believed the afterworld to be a complicated place of many levels. A childless man was doomed for all eternity to have low status no matter how rich. Without a son, it was difficult for him to be buried properly at all. So if an important man had no son or the child predeceased him, a *gale-gale* was carved instead and danced as his son. According to some, the skull of the dead man was fitted with a wooden body and a wig so it too could dance. At the end of the funeral ceremony, when much of the wealth of the dead man had been consumed in its execution, the puppet would be 'cannibalized' − another celebrated Batak institution − to make fertility charms.

One surviving example has a hollow head that can be filled with wet moss so the doll can even cry. And in the tourist hotels of Parapat, there is a *gale-gale* operator who believes his time has come. 'Break-dancing!' he whispered to me. 'I'm teaching it break-dancing. With stiff wooden arms it's ideal. All I need is to get on television and I'm made.'

———✥———

Jeremy Bentham sits in a wood and glass box on wheels in the Senior Common Room of University College, London. In his hand he carries an old hazel walking stick called Dapple. On his head rests a favourite hat. The expression on the face is that of a benign Farmer Giles, masking the smug crudeness of most of his opinions. The utilitarian philosopher devised the panopticon so beloved of post-modernists, a prison in which inmates are isolated but authority all-seeing. In death, however, the positions are reversed. When his folding doors are unclapped, it is now Bentham who is displayed to tippling academic inmates while he himself sees nothing.

When Bentham died in 1832, he had his body 'dressed' by Dr Southwood Smith, the surgeon. The 'body' is in fact of wax, using his skeleton as a mere armature. One wonders what was the point of the whole affair. His real head, shrunk to a mien of leering imbecility, is kept in a box at his feet. It is said that, on occasion, he is wheeled out to attend meetings, his contribution being not notably less than that of other board members.

In China, a mixed Buddhist-Taoist religion led to the preservation of celebrated priests by lacquering, varnishing or coating the body in clay or gold. Bodies were first preserved by being eviscerated and pickled in a sealed jar for several years. If, when the jar was opened, an uncorrupted body was found, it might be directly varnished and gilded and would then last for several centuries. Alternatively, the monk would be expected to co-operate by fasting before death to obligingly dry out his own body and reduce the finishing work required. In other Buddhist establishments – notably in Ipoh and Singapore – devout laymen may still have their ashes mixed with cement and a statue made of their original likeness, one substance, one form.

The usage recalls that proposed by Pierre Giraud, architect and thinker, in 1801. The bodies of the dead would be vitrified into an innocuous glass and poured into a mould in their likeness. Such images could be stored to provide an instructive gallery of fame.

Significantly, only the brain of Einstein was preserved, pickled in a jar, his intellect hijacked as a relic, the rest of the body sloughed off as an encumbrance. The brain of Lenin, it has recently emerged, was kept too as an adjunct of the embalmed body so that it might be studied and the source of its unique power established. After years of research a team of scientists were forced to admit that it was quite ordinary in every particular.

—⟨⟨⟩⟩—

Medieval theologians and lawyers fretted abstractly about time, continuity and eternity, the relation of persons to corporations, individuals to species, offices to their holders and sacred to secular in a way that produced the richest mix of wildly inconsistent and counter-intuitive ideas up to the days of modern theoretical physics. One notion that went into the semantic soup was that the relations between a corporation and its head were like those between a child and its guardian, hence the Church, for example, was a perpetual child. Another widespread metaphor was the body politic with its head and limbs. The body lived on though the individual limbs might change. In England, the head was the king, the limbs Parliament. Of course, when the 'head' itself died, the image became problematic.* The royal corpse required treatment in some way that overcame the break in continuity.

In 1135 and 1272 there were riots in England owing to the belief that when the king died, so too did 'the king's peace'. There was, quite simply, no law any more. Such a situation was not unique. In 1705 Bosman noted of Ouidah, Benin: 'As soon as the king's death is public, everybody steals from his neighbour as best

*Kantorowicz, 1957

he can . . . without anyone having the right to punish, as if justice died with the king.' This view of things was carefully anticipated in French royal ritual from the fourteenth century on, where the justices specifically were excused mourning because 'by the death of the king justice does not cease'.*

The new head that wore the crown raised another particularly acute problem. Was a king a king before he had been crowned; and what was the relation of crown to king? The French, until they adopted funeral effigies from the English, buried their royals with their crowns on to show that legally the king never died. Later, a new king might not even see the image of his predecessor as they both embodied the same kingship. Another answer given was that there were in fact *two* crowns, one visible, the other invisible. It was the latter – eternal and descended dynastically or from God – that conferred legitimacy.

From this ferment, the Tudors derived a very strange idea, that the king had not one body but two. 'For the King has in him two Bodies, viz., a Body natural and a Body politic. His Body natural (if it be considered in itself) is a Body mortal, subject to all Infirmities that come by Nature or Accident, to the Imbecility of Infancy or old Age, and to the like Defects that happen to the natural Bodies of other People. But his Body politic is a Body that cannot be seen or handled, consisting of Policy and Government, and constituted for the Direction of the People, and the Management of the public weal, and this body is utterly void of infancy, and old Age, and other natural Defects and Imbecilities, which the Body natural is subject to, and for this Cause, what the King does in his Body politic cannot be invalidated or frustrated by any Disability in his natural Body'.†

We would see here a mere metaphor for speaking about the distinction between office and incumbent but in Tudor times it was taken very literally. Thus Parliament was able to raise troops in the name of the king to fight the king and execute his body natural

*Kantorowicz, 1957:418
†Plowden, 1816

124

while retaining his immortal body politic. Oaths, on the other hand, had to be sworn to the body natural as the body politic had no soul.

At death, the two bodies separated – a process known technically as *demise*. The body natural was placed in a coffin, its decay screened from public gaze, the body politic was exhibited in the form of an effigy, dressed in the royal robes and crown and kept on top of the coffin until the burial. The procedure had classical precedents. At the death of Augustus, two effigies were made, one drawn in a triumphal chariot, the other – of gold – brought to the Senate. Other terracotta effigies of relatives and noble Romans surrounded him, testifying to his place in the pageant of Roman history whilst the awkwardly rotting body was hidden from sight.

In the Elizabethan view, the invisible body politic became visible and indisputable on death in a reversal that amused commentators at the time. For some years, it had been acceptable to use effigies in bishops' funerals and construct their tombs with two images. On top, that of the churchman in full regalia of office. Beneath, an image of the decaying flesh.

We tend to see these images as a warning about the vanity of earthly success, the emptiness of human affectation. At the time, echoing as they did the physical relationship of effigy to body, they were more likely to be seen as making an opposite statement about the eternity of episcopal office and dignity.

The monarch is apparently no longer held to have two bodies. But she nonetheless still has two birthdays, official and unofficial, and two religions, the Scottish and the English, depending on which country she happens to be in. No wonder she refers to herself as 'we'.

The British funerary effigies, the 'ragged regiment', linger on in the undercroft of Westminster Abbey. After their moment of glory, the funeral effigies were stripped of crown, sceptre and ornaments and went downhill fast, ending up as a peepshow to make a little money for the gentlemen of the choir. When Elizabeth I's true effigy went astray, they commissioned a beaky new one to keep the revenues up and subsequently added Pitt and

Lord Nelson for their commercial appeal. The French effigies
fared even worse. At the Revolution, along with statues of saints,
they were fed to the omnivorous guillotine.

With the English Restoration, the effigy was ousted from its
place on the coffin – this being filled by the more successful fiction
of the Crown – and reduced to simply standing about like an
embarrassed spectator at its own funeral. Charles II still makes
something of a leg but now seems merely to be playing Errol
Flynn rather badly. He's wax of course. The earlier pieces are of
wood or plaster covered with gesso, the bodies of wood, leather,
canvas, straw and padding.

The royals do not, on the whole, impress. The most striking
thing about depictions of them from the nineteenth century are
the glass cases, frosted with the elaborate graffiti etched by visitors'
jewels, great swirls and curlicues that would not look out of place
on a New York subway train. Only a few remain now on the glass
enclosing the Duke of Buckingham. Edward III is shown in the
uncomfortable pose of a man doing sit-ups, one side of the face
palsied by the first of the strokes that carried him off, stripped of
his wig and beard and his eyebrows 'made of the hair of a small
dog'. Bloody Mary, her wooden body* having now gone the way
of all flesh, has the eager face of those Christians who come round
knocking on doors. If she had received a better press would we
not see apple cheeks and roguish eyes? To read the character of the
dead from their effigies is as absurd as creating pictures of people
over the telephone and then complaining that they do not look
like their voices. Yet even the ancient stuffed parrot of the Duchess
of Richmond looks harassed and ill at ease. Anne of Denmark
(James I's wife) is full-breasted and spotty. Anne of Bohemia and
Catherine de Valois both look moronic, fit to be clapped up in a
tower rather than returned to care in the community. Catherine
was the wife of Henry V and her real body suffered an even more
inglorious fate than her effigy. Embalmed in 1437, owing to all
manner of operating difficulties, she was not finally buried until

*Hope, 1907

1878.* In the interim, her preserved corpse, kept in a box, became a tourist attraction. In 1668, she was kissed by Samuel Pepys. 'I had the upper part of her body in my hands, and I did kiss her mouth, reflecting upon it that I did kiss a Queene.'

The gem of the Abbey's collection is Henry VII, a superb plaster head, the neck corded and ravaged at the advanced age of fifty-two. It seems it was a death mask since a clotted eyebrow was caused by too much grease being spread over the hair of the corpse. It's a good honest face that looks you straight in the eye across the centuries, quintessentially British, unaffected, decent. Then you realize, actually . . . apart from the missing dimple, it's the spitting image of Kirk Douglas.

—◦◦◦—

It was pitch dark and a little eerie waiting outside the funeral caves on a moonless night. Mist was seeping up from the river and pouring down into the hollow like in a low-budget horror movie. The friend who had come with me had sprawled on the cooling rocks and was smoking silently, occasionally inflicting a series of sharp jerks on his neck in the way Indonesians insist is good for it. I was on my best behaviour. Any jokes about ghosts and I had been warned he would be haring off to his motorbike, abandoning me to a solitary walk home. The Torajans of Sulawesi still make almost life-sized effigies of nobles, *tau-tau*, to stand outside the tombs where their bones are housed and this – it seemed – was how you bought one. Over my shoulder there were whole ranks of them, standing erect on balconies, with semaphorically raised hands like royal families posing for photographers. 'One hand gives; one hand receives.' They wear clothes and hats and sport traditional hairstyles in tufty hair made of the inner bark of the *induk* palm.

My friend stiffened. His ears were sharper than mine. A figure

*Litten, 1992:41

127

slid on to the rock beside me, materializing from nowhere. Clad in black, all I could see was his white teeth when he smiled. We shook hands.

'I was afraid you would not come.'

It was odd. I felt perfectly safe here.

'The *tau-tau*,' he said. 'That's what we call them. *Tau* means 'man' so the reduplication could be a diminutive 'little man', or it could imply something like 'real, true, man'. There are different views.'

'You're a schoolteacher,' I said.

'I used to be a teacher.' He looked briefly annoyed. 'How did you know? Now I carve.'

'Did you carve any of these?' I indicated vaguely the looming figures above us.

'Some are old. Some I carved. Do you want a new one or an old one?'

'You must understand. I want two new ones, one male, one female, and I need the right documentation, all the stamps. This has to be official.'

'You are right. New ones are better, more exact. But ... most tourists want old ones. You do not have to be shy. It can be arranged. You know the heads and arms come off and you can pack them in your luggage. I have seen the auction prices in Holland. They are very expensive.'

The figures nowadays are increasingly naturalistic. They may wear glasses and have warts and wrinkles. Previously those for the higher nobles had simple geometric faces but showed tattoos. The style has changed because the carvers are sent to Bali for training. This is part of the consequence of their religion being nonsensically classed by the government as 'Hindu'. Never mind. At least it means it is now officially recognized and has protection.

'No this is government,' I said. 'They will be checked in Ujung Pandang. I don't want any trouble. It is forbidden to sell the old ones.'

I passed him a cigarette and in the flare of the match I saw a sharp-eyed, wiry man in his mid-forties. He sounded annoyed again.

'It is not for the government to say what we can do. Who do these figures belong to? They do not care about them. It is only for the tourists. They think if the figures are not on show, the tourists won't come.' His voice sank to a whisper. 'The ministry has hired me in the past to make fakes to put outside the tombs. Tourists can't tell the difference. Are you a Catholic or a Protestant?'

Modern Torajans increasingly join one of the smorgasbord of date-expired Christian churches exported from the West. In a country where your religion is on your identity card, only a criminal lunatic has no religion. The Catholics seem not to mind if their flock put up a figure as long as it is thought of in the right i.e. non-idolatrous way. Some Protestants allow participation in funeral feasts but draw the line at killing buffalo for the dead, others at setting up *tau-tau*. Some say the figure recalls the dead to memory, others that it replaces the decayed body, some indeed deny any link with the dead and call it a 'guardian' or a servant to wait on them in the next world.

'I'm a Protestant,' I simplified. 'What about you?'

'Me too.' We patted each other in religious solidarity.

'I heard some *tau-tau* were stolen from here last year.'

He sighed, took a deep breath and blew out smoke. 'You should not believe all you hear. Often the family want to sell them and cannot, or there is one old man who does not agree. So we arrange for the *tau-tau* to be 'stolen'. There is a man in town with contacts in Bali. He holds them for a month or two. If there is no trouble, he passes them on. You know that the statues have to be renewed from time to time or the dead get angry? So you buy a fine new one cheaply from me, sell the rotten, old one expensively to the foreigners and everyone is happy. The dead are happy. The living are happy. One hand gives; one hand receives. Children can go to school. Tax can be paid. But the government are not happy.'

It all sounded very reasonable, the cry of a living man resenting being 'museumized' for outsiders to come and photograph him. I knew that for the farmer, who looks up at the *tau-tau* as he labours in the rice-fields, they are increasingly problematic. He may well find them an embarrassing reminder of pagan days, yet be nervous also of neglecting the dead. It seemed our business was over. The carver-schoolteacher slid off the rock and stuck out a hand.

'Come back tomorrow. We can do this in daylight in front of the policeman. The more open we are, the more he will be angry and confused. Don't forget the photo.'

'Photo?'

'The face of the dead, so I can carve it.'

There are not many moments when you find yourself regretting that you don't carry the photographs of your enemies permanently on you. When I returned some days later, he had extemporized. 'Faces from the paper. I do not know who'. The woman was almost certainly Golda Meir, the man bore a striking resemblance to Prince Charles.

7

Fixed Abode:
Time, Place and Death

' "There's no sense in lying dead in Llanstephan," he said.
"The ground is comfy in Llangadock; you can twitch your legs
without putting them in the sea." '

Dylan Thomas (1914–53)

The Friends of Highgate Cemetery are dedicated to the preservation of genteel decay, and this is one graveyard that is alive and well. Volunteers can be seen most weekends in their green wellies stripping back the worst excesses of the foliage and damping down the ivy that breeds with proletarian enthusiasm. Cut back, but not too much, gently guide, but beware of spoiling character. It is like watching the British Raj moderating the 'excesses' of India. Inside the cemetery gates decay is presented not as putrescent rotting but as a process of gentrified patination.

The graves themselves are rife with masonry beasts. Paschal lambs and doves flaunt their innocence. The sleeping dog of Thomas Sayers, the pugilist, sits cheek-by-jowl with the nag of Queen Victoria's 'by appointment' horse-knacker. The lion, Nero, singular pride of George Wombewell, the menagerist, dozes as by a fireside. The great nineteenth-century cemeteries, where persons of quality were intended to stroll and appreciate the timeless beauties of art, are now redeemed by pressure groups as nature reserves, havens for *wild* animals and plants and proof that everything changes, even death. In Highgate the classic cornice is a nesting place for threatened species and the tour parties – led round by comfortingly dotty volunteers – are stalked by a pregnant black feral cat that ducks in and out of fractured mausolea like a familiar.

At the entrance, there is a great business with change and little tins of coins, demonstrating studied distaste for the things of Mammon. Books are on sale but no one quite knows the price. Money is all a little 'embarrassing'.

Restoration is piecemeal, at the mercy of individual grants and specific fund-raising drives, so that each new patch highlights the poignant ruin of the rest. The names of the famous are flaunted like the alumni of some public school, each reinforcing the notion that Highgate Cemetery is a good address. Even in the most individualist of cultures, the dead get ingested into something more general, here, the great procession of British history. The lesbian writer Radclyffe Hall, immured with her lover, is glossed as a 'feminist'. She has had a facelift, her arch freshly grouted by granite-faced supporters. A military man has had his cannons retouched.

Over the other side of the road, amongst the proletariat and their mentors, lie the people with headstones of reconstituted stone and plastic flowers. Karl Marx is next to Herbert Spencer, so that Marks and Spencer are fittingly, side by side.

The placing of the dead is never arbitrary. It is a clear act of classification and a statement of where they belong. Among the Nuer of Sudan, deformed dead babies are gently put down by the river and so returned to the hippos that are their real fathers, reallocated to the animal domain. In a similar act of character association Hugh Heffner is said to have spent a fortune to acquire the burial lot next to Marilyn Monroe.

In the West, since the Reformation, there has been an increasing separation of the living and the dead, extended nowadays to the living and those nearing death. While the world has always seen huge movements of people, as emigrants, refugees and deportees, it is not just the living who have to adjust to political change by moving. The dead too, especially the prominent dead, have their bodies shunted about to bring them into line with the new maps of the not-yet-dead and so authenticate them with the weight of history.

Frederick the Great has returned to a freshly defined Germany. General Sikorski has gone back to a newly independent Poland as a token of its democracy. The shrivelled heart of King Boris of Hungary has been prominently reburied to represent that country's re-emerging national identity from the faceless Eastern European bloc. The Romanovs of Russia might have been thought to have disappeared for ever. After all, they were shot, burned, doused with sulphuric acid and ground to dust by repeatedly reversing a truck over them. Now, minimal remains have been genetically identified by DNA analysis, using comparative samples provided by the Duke of Edinburgh, and there are plans to house their fragments and their reconstituted memory in a church, including tombs and a huge tourist complex on the site of their execution in the city of Ekaterinburg. Meanwhile Lenin's body, pure and incorruptible, but rumoured to be a mere fake in wax, has been withdrawn from public display in the Kremlin and seems destined for a humbler grave, following that of the discredited Stalin. The ousting of the untainted founder of the communist state from the heart of political power is clearly a powerful symbol of a change in his place within Russian life. The mummification of the body in essence reflected the mummification of ideology and the whole dead hand of the state. Its interment sanctions an official allocation to the past of much more than just his bones.

In China, the bones of the dead act as channels of *feng-shui*, forces of wind and water, that bring good or bad fortune. They become part of the active general landscape and their presence may be advanced as a reason for stopping a building or preserving a view. Interestingly, this is often optimistically mistranslated as the beginnings of a Western-style environmentalist movement in China.

Every immigrant group sooner or later faces the point where the bodies are no longer sent 'home' and so burial becomes an act of self-identification. An alternative is to bring 'home' to the dead. Since the diaspora, Jews have been ritually buried in soil from the Holy Land. Bags of it are still available for pouring over the dead, explaining those otherwise enigmatic medieval descriptions – prone to misunderstanding – of prominent figures as 'merchants of dirt'.

In the West, the dead are supremely matter out of place and undertakers offer a round-the-clock service promising to get them out of the house within hours. In traditional Chinese usage, it was important at all costs to avoid a death within the domestic space. Amongst the Cantonese, special buildings were provided to which the sick would be carried so they could actually die there. Until quite recently these could still be seen in Sago Lane, Singapore. The Maasai carried this so far as not only to remove the dying to the bush but also to forbid the killing of so much as a mouse inside the house or the pursuit of enemies within a compound during a raid.

The spatial location of a tomb tells much about where it is placed on other cultural maps. So in Samoa, the presence of ancestral tombs is the best evidence there is about perpetual land ownership. The declining popularity of burial amongst ourselves says much about our reduced rootedness in one place. In the early days of Christianity in England, should someone die whilst undergoing the fairly lengthy rites of conversion, they would be buried with their feet outside the hallowed ground of the cemetery and their head inside, showing where they came from and where they were 'headed'. Up until the nineteenth century it was still common even in Northern Europe for bodies to be exhumed once the flesh had decayed, so that ownership of a grave was for a short time only. During the nineteenth century, horrifically detailed public enquiries exposed the scandal of scarcely buried, putrescent bodies being dug up from London graveyards and chopped to pieces. Under the new arrangements instituted then, rights in the grave would become the ultimate in eternal freehold so that we are now horrified at the disturbing of bodies and even seek to inhibit access to shipwrecks lying several miles down at the bottom of the Atlantic. By a curious inversion we now see the dead as guarantors of the basic rights of the living, asking 'If even the dead can be "disturbed" what chance have the living to hang on to private property?'

Tombs often take the form of a house and those who live and sleep under one roof should be buried together. Most of our knowledge of Etruscan architecture comes, bizarrely, from tombs that mirror the forms of ordinary houses. It is as if our knowledge of nineteenth-century London was constructed solely from the remains of Highgate Cemetery. Yet, as with all images, the tomb as house can be interpreted with different degrees of explicitness. In our own houses, we normally expect only one sexually active couple. When children reach sexual maturity – the mark of adulthood – they are expelled. It is only according to the dramatic licence of soap operas that several generations continue to live dynastically beneath the same roof. For us, the family tomb has a whiff of post-mortem incest. We are not alone in this. The Sakalava of Madagascar forbid couples between whom incest prohibitions are in force to visit tombs together.

The metaphor reached an interesting point a few years ago in one London borough when there was agitation for women-only and lesbian-only graveyards. For some, the next life should consist entirely of people of our own sort.

It is not only the living who may be polluted by the dead; so can the dead. When the Antaimanambondro of Madagascar bury their dead in trenches, they are careful to remove bodies already there and lay the fresh ones at the bottom before they are replaced, lest these should be contaminated by the new arrivals. There is hierarchy even in death.

—◦◦◦—

135

After being flung from the walls Jezebel was eaten by dogs; the Old Testament leaves us in no doubt that this was a fitting end for a wanton woman. Being eaten by animals was a suitable insult, an act of reclassification as carrion. Less deserved was the fate of the Duc d'Orleans. When his heart was removed for pious interment in 1723, his pet Great Dane leaped across the room and enthusiastically devoured a good quarter of it.

Being 'food for worms' is still the worst way we have of imagining death and we also touchily class carrion as inedible and so avoid secondary cannibalism just as we legislate against 'twice sold food'. Others go further. The nineteenth-century naturalist Charles Waterton earned himself a reputation as an eccentric by forbidding the consumption of ducks on his estate after his death. The logic was that ducks ate worms, worms would have eaten him, therefore anyone eating ducks might indirectly be consuming his own flesh.

In Old English literature, the fate of the loser was to be devoured by the 'beasts of battle', ravens and wolves, a fearful mark of having no descendants, of the collapse of the social world, of being cosmically alone – dying a 'bad death'.

Christianity homed in on the notion that Man was made in the image of God, a cover under which respect for the body could be instilled into the proceedings. Yet the Maasai placed their dead in the bush in order to be consumed by scavengers and predators. On the north-west coast of Canada ravens dined on Kwakiutl cadavers. The Malabar Towers of Silence were one of the major hits of nineteenth-century European tours of India. Here the remains of Parsees were exposed to be eaten by birds of prey and thus avoid the defiling of water, air and fire. The bones were swept into a central pit. They say that once vultures have tasted brain, they are reluctant to settle for lesser cuts of flesh so that it could take a long time for bodies to disappear.

By their handling of the space allotted for the dead, different cultures retie the knot between Man and Nature at different points. For generations, there was a running battle in the Church of England to prevent the grazing of the parson's livestock in the

136

graveyard as they were in some sense consuming the dead. It ended abruptly in the late eighteenth century when sheep fitted quite happily into the notion of the rustic graveyard as a return to the pastoral. The Marquis de Sade was a pioneer of this, arranging for his grave to be dug in the forest at Malmaison and planted with acorns so as to be totally consumed by trees. For us, still, to be devoured by plants is all very well − even poetic − by animals unpleasant. Thus, in a sense, we all die vegetarian deaths.

A concern with place can involve other issues. The Northern Sudanese villagers studied by Janice Boddy have a culture strongly concerned with 'closure' of space and the body.* It is significant that these villagers both prefer to marry close kin and practise Phaoronic circumcision that 'seals' the female body by removing the labia and stitching closed the opening after each birth. The outside is deeply threatening. A distinction is made between porous water vessels that sweat and the totally sealed, glazed, *gulla* in which the batter of unleavened bread is soaked. A woman's womb is likened to the leakproof *gulla* and the process of gestation to the making of bread. Similarly a house has all its entrances watched, like a woman's body. All these perceived similarities result in special rules for the placing of the dead. So a miscarried foetus is buried in a *gulla* vessel *inside* the house. A stillborn baby is wrapped and buried near the *outer* wall of the house i.e. metaphorically outside the body but not in the outside world. Pots, houses and burials offer a way of collapsing all sorts of problems associated with dangerous leakage and help control the living bodies of women.

Some places are death-free zones. It is not normally possible to die legally in the Houses of Parliament, since constitutionally, it is a royal palace where death must be certified by a royal surgeon. No such person actually exists at the Palace of Westminster. The body of a deceased MP is therefore conveyed to a makeshift mortuary to

*Boddy, 1982

the right of St Stephen's Gate and will be registered as having been found dead on arrival at nearby St Thomas's Hospital.

It was not the Hammer House of Horror that invented the driving of stakes through human corpses. Until 1823, British suicides were often buried at crossroads similarly impaled – apparently to avoid the spirit wandering. The last on record was John Morland who in that year murdered Sir Warwick Bampfylde in Montague Square and later killed himself. He is to be found at the crossroads outside Lord's cricket ground, now – confusingly – beneath a war memorial to the Glorious Dead.

The crossroads is a powerful spatial idea worldwide, the crossing of two paths, one spot with two simultaneous locations, potentially everywhere and actually nowhere. After the law changed in 1823, British suicides might be buried in unconsecrated ground within a churchyard but only in darkness between the hours of nine and midnight.

In a Christian graveyard, bodies are buried with the head to the West and the feet to the East but the basic division has always been between North and South. The left-hand side of the altar (north) was called the gospel side for sinners, the right-hand (south) was the epistle side for the righteous.* So, traditionally, the unclean – such as a woman being 'churched' after childbirth – entered by the north and exited by the south. The unclean dead were buried to the north of the graveyard. In later times, burial occurred inside the church and a second hierarchy distinguished the rich who were near the altar from the poor who were near the door.

———<small>ᘒᘒᘒ</small>———

The distinction between signs of mourning and memorials is untenable cross-culturally for memorials do not have to be fixed in

*Puckle, 1926:150

one place. The scars inflicted on your own body in mourning may be a permanent memorial to the dead. In Hawaii it was not unusual to tattoo the name and date of death of a prominent person on one's body and become a sort of ambulant living tombstone.

Even in eighteenth- and nineteenth-century Britain, the bereaved were expected to follow a prolonged programme of deep and then half-mourning that introduced death into all areas of social life and involved a whole range of special material props. In the early Victorian period, a year's full mourning was held suitable for a dead spouse or parent, nine months for grandparents, six for brother or sister and three for aunt or uncle. Mourning rings and blackened swords were worn. Even ladies' fans were recruited to show the bearer's relationship with death. Those with white leaves mounted on black sticks would point to their still being in half-mourning, often long after the departure of the relevant family member so that they too became a sort of living monument, carrying the dead around with them.

Some cultures erase the dead entirely so that forgetting them is the proper thing to do. They stress the processes by which the dead are to be replaced. The whole of lowland South America is strikingly unmarked by ancestral cults.* Even in Africa the Mbuti pygmies refuse to allude to or recall the dead at all, their very names are forbidden to be spoken.

Among the Jivaro, the rotting of the body will be described graphically in song as part of the systematic destruction of the individual that frees his identity for someone else, for it is known that there can never be more than a certain number of persons at one time. So the dead must be stripped of face, identity and name for re-use by the living. The famous require more mourning work than the unknown as they have greater individuality to be dismantled. This, too, is why those killed by headhunters are recalled with such rage and bitterness. They cannot undergo the processes of mourning that alone allow them to be forgotten.

*Taylor, 1993

Many monuments lump together the dead and even the living and the dead. In London, the 'glorious dead', the military dead of the Commonwealth, are commemorated by the Cenotaph, at the heart of government, a tomb that contains no actual body and so all bodies. In many other European countries a structure with a body but no name performs a similar function. In the United States there is the Tomb of the Unknown Soldier that contains unidentified representatives of the various war dead. Although the decision was taken in 1973 to add a Vietnam 'Unknown' to it, it took ten years, following enormous advances in forensic medicine and medical documentation, to locate one who was truly unidentifiable. The dead retained their individuality and so could not be satisfactorily generalized.

There is some slight confusion as to who is officially commemorated by the Cenotaph. Is it just the dead of the two World Wars or all wars? The defining image is death as self-sacrifice. They died, we are told, that we might live. Heroism is one way of reconciling the individual and the collective in a culture that stresses the value of the former over the latter. It works through a sort of twisted logic, asserting that their supreme individuality lay in an individual act of self-denial.

Every year, there is a ceremony on Remembrance Day at which it is declared that they will not be forgotten. Remembrance is the measure of their heroism and our gratitude and in a culture that believes in neither afterlife nor reincarnation, memory is the only place left for identity to go. In 1993, however, it was mooted that the ceremony might not now be repeated as there were few living survivors who *did* remember the dead. They were being forgotten.

Representatives of all areas of public life are required to appear at the Cenotaph and lay wreaths: the forces, the Church, the civilian services, the government, the royal family, youth movements, old soldiers, Commonwealth diplomats. Care is taken to include Scottish, Welsh and Irish music. It is a great statement of the unity and solidarity of the living and the dead, a 'lumping together' rite of solidarity. Soviet monuments concentrated on achieving the same end by bringing together marriage and death through the obligatory visit of newly-weds to their local war memorial.

Noticeably, however, hierarchy is strictly observed. As elsewhere, the levelling effect of death on servicemen of unknown rank, name and nationality goes hand-in-hand with infinite discriminations of status among the living. It is often the function of memorials to reintroduce hierarchy into death so the insistence of Saudis that their royals should be buried beneath an undistinguished pile of rocks seems to us bombastic self-abasement like Greta Garbo scrubbing her own floors or the Pope washing feet. Here, High Commissioners lay wreaths in the order in which their countries gained independence and distinction creeps into the offerings made. The Queen opts for a wreath containing black silk poppies, the fragility of youthful life – marked by fragile flowers – being sacrificed to other richer symbolisms. The Prince of Wales gives one including ostrich feathers, the Foreign Secretary – on behalf of the Overseas Territories – one of 'exotic leaves' and Hong Kong bamboo plucked from the Royal Botanic Gardens. The seeds of division are already there through the very need to identify and represent groups, a fact even more apparent in the American Vietnam War Veterans' Memorial.

The memorial, a wall of stark austerity, consists of simple black marble blocks. Inevitably, it is located in Washington where the American corporate identity lives. The monument's undoing began with the decision to have inscribed on it the names of every individual American who died in the conflict. Controversy immediately sprang up around the decision whether to include those still 'missing in action'.

The wall has become not just a memorial but a shrine. People take rubbings of the names of relatives and leave offerings which are 'archivised'. Official records are kept of events at the wall and the objects left – 30,000 to date – are stored in a government warehouse in Maryland. They include medals, guns, ladies' underwear, a teddy bear, cigarettes, Zippo lighters, letters of notification of death – even an inner tube from a bicycle wheel. It has become an American Wailing Wall but rather less well administered. At the

Jerusalem Wall faxes can be delivered by the Israeli Post Office and poked directly between the stones. In deference to geographical egalitarianism, a half-sized replica of the Vietnam memorial tours the country and elicits its own offerings, now stored in another government warehouse. Such giving by many who may be devoid of religious faith refutes many of the pompous assumptions of anthropologists about gifts and exchange. Here there is not necessarily any receiver. The very fact that receipt is doubtful enhances the gift. It pleases *simply* to give.

President Reagan hoped to cure Americans of any lingering feeling of national dishonour about Vietnam when in 1984 he commissioned an heroic sculpture. Like a title to a painting it would direct how the names on the memorial wall should be 'read'. It shows three US servicemen, one black, one white, one arguably Hispanic, in a comradely pose. The medium here is at war with the message. To show that ethnicity does not matter, each of the soldiers must be racially different so that they can then be shown to be the same. Yet it is hard to show race in a bronze that obliterates differences of skin colour.

It caused a scandal by not including – amongst other groups – women, seeming to maintain the convention by which men may fall in war but women are only fallen. So yet another sculpture was commissioned from a female sculptor, showing three nurses and a wounded soldier in a posed creation that has been likened to a still from the television series *MASH*. And so it grows. The need to explicitly include all groups, as in the credits at the end of a movie, leads to a dismantling of national identity in the very act of its celebration.

—◦◦◦—

Sometimes it is less the dead that are recalled than death itself. Skeletons in medieval wall paintings warn of the inevitability of death. Muslims are urged to think of death at least once a day as

142

Philip of Macedon (d. 336 BC) is said to have retained a servant to remind him daily, 'You too one day will die'.

Death is not just a matter of place. It is also a matter of time. Control of the time of one's death is a major factor in the interpretation of it as good or bad. In many cultures, death is involved in the cycle of the seasons and people may not officially die, or at least no mortuary ceremonies may be held, until the appropriate stage of agriculture.

Dividing the death rites into two parts, the first dealing with the messy processes of bodily decomposition, the second with the ritual process of reallocating the dead, allows mortality to be tidied up according to cultural notions of the right time to die. So again and again in ethnographic descriptions we find that funerals only happen at a particular time of the year and involve two stages.

The medieval notion of a good death was by definition a gradual one. Sudden death was bad. It prevented the making of proper arrangements and the drawing of lessons. Montaigne (1533–92) shocked the world when he claimed that he wished to go suddenly while digging cabbages. Time and again the early medieval period restates the proposition that the good man *knows* when his end is nigh and arranges for it to happen in the right place. Hindus similarly stress that an ideal death is both an act of will and an act of knowledge.

For the Victorians, death should be organized as a meaningful tableau, mourners tastefully arranged around the bed of the dying. But, as Nigel Llewellyn shows, in former times, the British began the process of dying long before the deathbed was reached and in post-Reformation England about a third of funeral monuments were erected for people still alive.*

In modern life, death is less a cosmological than a social problem. The Western 'good' death has become the opposite of that common elsewhere in the world. Good death comes suddenly and without warning, the heart attack at the ninth hole, and disrupts

*Llewellyn, 1991

the flow of life as little as possible. Nowadays, we measure the importance of a death by the disturbance it makes in the course of life *after* it. When Queen Victoria died most of Britain and much of the Empire were plunged into mourning. When the mother of the Zulu ruler Chaka ('the great female elephant with small breasts') died in the early nineteenth century, he imposed sexual continence on the whole nation for a year and threw out the alternation of seasonal activities by forbidding cultivation and the drinking of milk for three months.

In Western culture such a sense of time comes less from the alternation of the seasons but the regularity of the TV schedules. That is the real reason everyone remembers where they were when Kennedy was shot. Television programmes were interrupted.

⟞᭡᪣᪣᭡⟝

It was three in the morning in London and the phone was ringing. At that hour you answer with your heart in your mouth. Vague twanging noises and crashing waves came down the line, then a voice said 'Pong' and I knew who it was. *Pong* is a term of respect in Torajaland. Its use in relation to me was a standing joke.

About five years earlier I had organized a Torajan exhibition in a museum in the middle of London. We had imported a container of wood, bamboo and rattan – everything you needed to build a traditional ricebarn – and with it came a family of Torajan carvers and painters who built it from scratch. They had constituted a history of Toraja in miniature. The grandfather, Nenek Tulian, was a high priest of the old religion and spoke Torajan. The next generation were Christians and spoke Indonesian as well. The grandson, Johanis, wore jeans, worshipped nothing but the US dollar and studied English at the university. It was him on the phone.

'I am calling you from the middle of the forest,' Johanis said, 'to say that grandfather is dead. Will you come? You promised when we were in London. Wait . . .'

There was a click and suddenly I heard the voice of Nenek the grandfather chanting, bardic, melodious, the voice pitched high, intoning an ancient religious poem from beyond the grave. Abruptly, he broke off and said in Indonesian, 'You, my friend in London. Come again even if I am dead.' Another click.

'He just came out with that at a ceremony days before he died. I was recording it,' Johanis said.

'Why were you recording it?' I asked. 'Did you finally decide to take over the succession, to become a priest?'

He laughed. 'Nooo. I took another path. I decided to study anthropology like you. I turned Nenek into my thesis.' Then with the heartlessness of the young, he added, 'Don't worry, I got all the data I needed before he died.'

'I will come,' I said. 'Write and tell me when. You can't bury him now. It's spring.'

There was a chuckle. 'Spring? In the valleys it's spring but up here it's winter. You'll understand when you get here. Come now.'

Suddenly something occurred to me. 'How can you call me from the middle of the forest?'

'I'm at the satellite receiving station. I have a cousin who works here so we come to watch the Thai porno movies and use the phone free. It's family.'

Funerals are something the Torajans do very well, sometimes exhausting the wealth of a whole generation in a few short days. As elsewhere, when death is marked by large-scale consumption or destruction of property, riches are simultaneously shunted into the celestial bank account of the deceased, family status is hitched up and the debts of years are repaid. There may be hundreds of guests, dozens of buffalo killed, whole temporary villages built like film sets and burned to the ground afterwards. Prestige is more enduring than concrete. The body of the deceased is sometimes kept for years in the house, wrapped in layers of absorbent cloth – by tradition not embalmed though nowadays some cheat and use formalin – while sufficient resources are mobilized for a proper

145

send-off. It was always assumed that 'modernisation' would kill off lavish funerals. Instead, cash from the tourist trade has fuelled a sort of ritual inflation.

At a typical Torajan funeral, guests are received at the gate in groups, bearing their gifts of buffalo or – small change – pigs and cloth. In return they are given betel nut, cigarettes and the special sugary cakes that are the token of Torajan hospitality. The men dress in headhunting outfits – complete with furry hats with metal buffalo horns – and greet guests with disconcerting whoops and feigned prods with their spears. Once heard, the Torajan battle cry is never forgotten. Palm wine and whisky flow freely and they sing haunting songs to lament and praise the dead. Schoolchildren are nowadays drafted in to tootle bamboo flutes, to the annoyance of elders since flutes are properly for life not death.

In all, Torajan funerals are jolly affairs where the old meet to rake over the past, drink and dance. The young, meanwhile, flock to them simply to meet one another and sidle away for trysts in the forest. 'If there were no funerals,' one told me cheerfully, 'no one would ever get married.'

On my arrival in Sulawesi, Johanis looked unhappy. 'Father,' he said, 'there are two things I must say that you will not like.' Since when had he called me Father? This must be serious.

'First there is a death in the valley and we must go today. Daud the tour operator – you remember him? His father is dead so this will be the biggest funeral of the year. He will bring his tourists to it and sell them tickets to get in – giving with the right hand and taking with the left.' He assumed the pose of a funeral effigy. 'You must go to show respect. Second, Nenek is already in the tomb.'

'What! You mean I've come all this way for nothing?'

He held up a hand. 'The family declared that Nenek had con-verted to Christianity at the end, which meant that they could avoid all those expensive ceremonies and put him in a concrete tomb with a cross on top.' I could not believe it. He had told me he would never change his religion. 'Now we have to take him out of the Christian tomb and put the bones in a rock tomb in the traditional way. The family has nothing more to say. You will buy

146

a buffalo and save them the expense of feeding the guests. Nenek can go to his rest in peace. That is why you were meant to come.'

At Daud's funeral we were greeted at the entrance to the village by elegant girls clad in clinging dresses with gold flowers in their hair. Girls are transformed by traditional dress. In everyday life, they wear their skirts too short and their make-up too thick. In ethnic dress they are all silk-whispering virgins. Gongs boomed. They bowed low, eyes modestly averted, 'Welcome ... oh, it's *you!*' They giggled and flashed wanton looks at Johanis. We were led over to greet the family and offered coffee. Daud sat down with us briefly, dispensed cigarettes and matches in a display the length of his leg and made a joke about being a modern Torajan, cutting the throats of Toyota vans instead of buffalo. He pointed, fingers politely splayed. 'That man is a famous inventor. He studied in America.' The inventor was waved over and showed us his latest creation.

All over Torajaland you see tourists struggling with three-foot-high Y-shaped packages. Inside there could be only one thing, a model Torajan house. Houses are crucial to Toraja identity. Everyone has to have a carved and painted noble house in the hills where he really 'belongs', where his festivals are held, where he sends money even if he has to live in a shack in the city. The houses with their great curved roofs perch lightly on the earth, streams purling around their feet, looking as if they might take off at any minute. The models are fine things too but cumbersome.

'See,' said the inventor. He held out a typical model house, withdrew a single sliver of wood and the whole thing collapsed gently like a soufflé in a draught. 'You carry it like this. When you get home, you push it back in and...' The house rose again in all its inconvenient glory. 'Wah! I expect to become a millionaire.'

On the way back, following a serpentine path over hills and teetering over slimy, moss-covered bridges, we called in at Nenek's house. A perfectly good road led the same way but there was a sound reason for our detour. 'We have to do this because of the new rice,' said Johanis. 'In the old days, you had one crop of rice a year. Now you get two, maybe three. Rice is life, and death must

147

not be mixed with life, so we hold the funerals in autumn.' But it is the rice that decides the season.' He pointed to a hill, lurid with sprouting rice shoots. Nothing can match the vivid green of new rice. 'Over there, you see, it is spring and we must not tread there on our way to a funeral.' In another direction, he indicated a stand of tall stalks. 'Over there, it is summer – no death. But over here . . .' He snatched up a stalk of rice already stripped of its ears from the field we were wading through, 'autumn, so alright for funerals. It's crazy. Now we have to find you a second-hand buffalo to buy. Remember to get a receipt.' He gave me an accountant's look. 'You can use it against tax.'

'Oh, right.'

At the funeral Johanis finished his speech in high Torajan, waving his spear about and then he swaggered back grinning.

'I said you gave this buffalo for Nenek. If they killed it that was good. If they kept it that was good too. I did some fancy high-priest stuff – poems – and said you gave it for the Queen of England. They liked that.'

We sat in front of Nenek's carved house in the sunshine, remembering, talking about the things he had said and done. Like all builders, he never quite got around to finishing his own house. The roof was lopsided. It looked as if you only had to remove one plank to make the whole thing collapse like the inventor's model.

A mile or so away, you could see the tombs pecked laboriously into the granite rockface. I thought of the natural caves over the mountains at Londa that had a similar function. I had been taken in by a little boy of about five who had picked up a skull. 'Here's my grandad,' he had said matter-of-factly.

'How do you know?'

He pointed to the forehead. 'Here. You see I wrote his name in biro.' A thanatologist would call that the triumph of individualism.

To one side, the buffalo was already being boiled down in a huge cauldron, the sort cannibals in cartoons use. The horns would be put on the house front. Laughing Torajans stood around with swords and spears swallowing great draughts of hot stock from the pot. An old man was sitting in a car seat on the ground. Johanis indicated him. 'Yesterday he could hardly get down from his house. Today he is young again. That's meat!'

The family had imported a Catholic priest, in glasses and with Brylcreemed hair, who gave it to them hot and strong on the subject of idolatry with lots of Bible-waving. Impertinently, I thought, he also made a collection. Everyone watched. Would I give? I gave. The buffalo was brought round, great, chewy, grey slugs of meat. Would I eat?

'He will not eat it,' said someone. 'He's a Christian.'

'If he gave it, he can eat it.'

'If you give something you should not eat it yourself.' Eyes burned into me.

Suddenly, one of the girls was there with – of all things – a plate of chips. 'Johanis has explained to us what white men eat,' she whispered for all to hear. He winked at me from afar.

A man came up with a clipboard and flashed a badge officiously.

'Excuse me sir. Are you the owner of this buffalo?'

'Er. Yes.' I had bought it mere hours ago.

He cleared his throat and consulted the board.

'First, there is the matter of three years' unpaid buffalo tax on this beast. Then there is the government's sacrifice tax for the negative investment of positive national economic resources. Then. . .'

Johanis led him away, whispering in his ear with passionate intensity, grinning back at me. The man tucked his clipboard under his arm and walked off. Later I would see him haring across the fields, a buffalo leg hooked over one shoulder. 'Family,' shrugged Johanis.

Then it was time to move Nenek's body, no awe or ritual, a matter of 'You hold that while I break the door with this crowbar.' As always, only men were involved but there were crowds of little boys, mouths open, taking it all in, peering, picking their noses.

We pulled the coffin out of the house into the sunshine. His bright green plastic flip-flops were – as though miraculously – preserved. In Western tombs, I thought, you would get not just bones but plastic teeth and breast implants, the body reduced to caricature sexual allure. Ants had nested in Nenek's skull and when we opened the lid they swarmed out to attack the mourners. A child was sent off to fetch a can of insecticide, appropriately named 'Doom', while the men all joined hands and twirled counter-clockwise in a booming death chant. Then the body was tightly wrapped in cloth, slung from a pole and zigzagged across the fields to avoid the green islands of growing rice.

I had once tried to keep up with Nenek through the mountains as he hopped like a goat from rock to rock. I had failed then and I failed even in death for the carriers ran at tremendous speed to the rock face a couple of miles away. Behind me, I heard the village head say, 'I'll ask the white man to pay for a swimming pool for the village.'

The tombs had been hacked in the granite a hundred feet or more above the ground. Torajans come from all over Asia to put the bones of their dead in these tombs, swarming up single bam-boo poles at huge risk. Every few years they take the bones out and rewrap them. Nenek's body was one of three being inserted that day and a spontaneous race developed between bearers of the three bereaved families, young men leaping on to the bundles of bones and riding them like rodeo broncos with whoops and yelps. Nenek won. Suddenly from above there burst a wave of howls and oaths. Looking up, we fell silent. Ghosts? No. Inside was a wasps' nest, the next moment flicked joyfully on to the squealing crowd below.

Johanis draped an arm around my shoulder and looked out over the lush valley. Huge storks were circling peacefully over the sun-lit mountains where the rice was germinating. 'Now Nenek too goes back to the spring,' he said, 'and makes the rice grow. Safe journey, Nenek.'

'Yes. Safe journey.'

'When you die,' said Johanis, 'I will come to your funeral. I enjoy a good funeral.'

8

Metaphors We Die By

'Human life most nearly resembles iron. When you use it, it
wears out. When you don't, rust consumes it.'
Marcus Porcius Cato (234–149 BC)

In the nineteenth century, on the former slave plantations of the American south, workers were seen placing broken pots on graves. When asked by white overseers for their reasons, they spoke of keeping the dead from coming back.* Their questioners already had their own ideas of what black religion was about so they ignored what they were told and saw the pots as 'offerings to the ancestors', i.e. a means of establishing contact with the dead. Yet in later years, the pottery on graves was replaced or supplemented by stopped clocks, set either to the time of death or just before midnight. This suggests that the pots were being used to draw a line in time just as the clocks were.

Death does not just exist. In order to have coherence and to find its place, it has to be integrated into a wider scheme of things. The location of death in circular flow charts of essences and such-like is one way to do this. Another is to tie it in with the seasons. Yet another is to imagine death as being *like* something else that is more readily accessible. It is a commonplace of anthropology that Westerners think about society with models drawn from natural science — statistics, classes, probabilities — whereas other peoples

*Valch, 1978

think about the natural world with models drawn from society – animals as relatives, weather as temperament etc.

Yet the – to us – odd ways that pots are used in African traditions show that pottery can provide equally technological ways of thinking about the body and death. So in Africa, pottery is more than something you cook with or use to carry water. It is something to think with, bringing together biological, technological and social change in a single metaphor. The irreversibility of a broken vessel offers a way of speaking of the irreversibility of human time, the change from living to dead. The ritual smashing of pottery creates a clean break between the two. So among the Asante of Ghana, breaking a pot on a man's head was thought to lead inexorably to his death. On the other hand, taking a fragment of broken pot, grinding it down and incorporating it into a new vessel can be a way of talking about reversing time or reincarnation.

So around the world, death ceremonies often involve the smashing of pots, just as ceremonies of marriage and life involve their creation. The West African midwife commonly doubles up as the potter while it is her husband, the blacksmith, who buries the dead.

In Africa, when some old men tired of trying to get me to understand reincarnation and the notion of the body as a vessel of spirit, they finally organized an outing to the local brewery, a place that held much the same position in their thought as the Garden of Eden might in ours. From here, glamorously excluded by a security fence, you could see returned bottles through a plate glass window, entering via one door, whirling from machine to machine, gliding magically along a production line, being endlessly refilled with squirting beer, re-labelled and pushed out through another door for shipment to a thirsty world. Men watched this ballet, transfixed, for hour after hour.

'Life, death, spirit and body. Now you have *seen*,' they said.

Other Chaga myths tell of reversible death. In olden days when a human died, he split apart with a bang like a calabash. But the

152

relatives came and sewed him back together again and he stood up whole and healthy. When an old woman was nearing her death, she called her children and said to them, 'Now I am going to die. Now choose the manner of the death that you want, my sons. Do you want to die and split like a calabash that can be mended or do you want to smash to pieces like a clay pot?' They answered, 'We want to smash to pieces like a clay pot.'

'Oh Woe!' cried the old woman. 'If you had said you wanted to split like a calabash, you would have been mended again, but how can you mend a smashed pot?'

So now Man is prey to a death that cannot be reversed.*

—◦◦◦—

The Dowayo of Cameroon see death as like circumcision. They have a particularly harsh form of male circumcision, peeling the penis for virtually its whole length. It literally sorts the men from the boys. Should a man attain maturity but die uncircumcized he is buried as a child or a woman. It is through circumcision that a man gains the most important male friends in his life, the men who joke with him, the men he was cut with. It provides a way of seeing many kinds of change.

The Dowayos describe circumcision as taking something ambiguously male and female – a boy – and removing part so that it is strengthened, purified and improved. Each year, the first millet is threshed to circumcision songs and through this process, female fruit becomes active male seed. Dead bodies have their skulls removed with a miming of circumcision. They are threatened with knives and menaced with genital cutting. In this way, a dead man or woman is made into an ancestor, strengthened, purified, improved and now capable of fertilizing women and giving children.

While Dowayos transform the gender of seed through circum-

*Gutmann, 1909:124

153

cision, seed itself can be a useful metaphor. A common medieval riddle asks what it is that must die in order to live. The answer to this, too, is a seed, so using it to deal not with the mutual implication of male and female but life and death.

The Christian liturgy flirts with it in the following passage, recommended reading for the funeral service in the Church of England Alternative Service Book:

> But someone will ask, 'How are the dead raised? With what kind of body do they come?' You foolish man! What you sow does not come to life unless it dies. And what you sow is not the body which is to be, but a bare kernel, perhaps of wheat or of some other grain. But God gives it a body as he has chosen, and to each kind of seed its own body. So it is with the resurrection of the dead. Corinthians, 15.

The Greek Orthodox service presses the point home more firmly with the dreadful words, 'the earth that fed you, now shall eat you,' as the mourners consume mixed fruits, nuts and seeds around the grave.

But the vegetable image that is most invoked seems to be that of brevity and demise. Death is the Grim Reaper. 'The days of Man are but as grass: he flourishes like a flower of the field; when the wind goes over it, it is gone...' (Psalm 103). After all, what are given at funerals are *cut* flowers doomed to swiftly wither. Until the Victorians developed the language of floral wreaths, sprigs of rosemary were cast into the open grave or it was later strewn with evanescent, fragile blooms before being permanently planted with sturdy evergreens.

The flower image finds its apotheosis in the epitaphs for children of the 'Budded in earth; blossomed in heaven' type and the carnation petit-point of wreaths – 'To Mum', quite literally, said with flowers. As faith in the afterlife continues to wither, there has been a veritable explosion of the use of cut flowers. No place of death now goes unmarked, indeed unobliterated, with flowers – a road accident, a fire, a house where the police have been digging for a body. It is a sort of claim for equal air time for the undistin-

154

guished dead. I once noticed the window of one London pub stacked with aluminium-papered sprays of petrol-station flowers. A residual Christian sense lurked in the nightlight that sputtered before them. An attached label seemed to cover all possible moral positions and idioms. 'Pray forgiveness,' it read, 'for the murdering bastard who cut you down.'

'It is strange to the European observer to see how harvest home, an occasion of rejoicing and church festival among ourselves, sets Dobu into concentration on the dead of the year, on ritual surrounding death.'* The sign of this is the baskets of yams from the dead man's land being carried all over the island to his sister's children. They cannot be eaten by his own children since links are traced through women and a man and his children belong to a different group or *susu*, 'milk'. The yams belong to his sister's children who are his heirs, for people and yams are thought of according to the same model.

A woman, her brothers and her children belong to one *susu*; her husband belongs to different *susu*. A village consists of a group of related *susu*, who are 'brothers' and 'sisters' to each other – therefore not marriageable – but who are thought to be attractive, slightly incestuous lovers, favourite partners for adultery.

A man or woman may only cultivate yams from seed handed down through their own *susu*, though anyone's land can be used. Similarly, children always belong to the mother's group though they are raised alternating back and forth between the marriage partners' villages. Husband and wife cultivate separately since you cannot grow yams from another *susu*'s seed and their growth involves magic also handed down according to the lines of the *susu*. People without seed cannot marry and marriage itself is marked by the mother-in-law pushing a digging stick into a boy's hand and telling him to get stuck in. Yams are really transformed people that wander about at night and they can be enticed from

*Fortune, 1932:18

155

other people's gardens just as other people's spouses can be enticed and seduced.

In the centre of the village stands the mound containing the dead, the group from which you have sprung and to which you will return. Like a vast yam mound, it is a symbol of a desirable security, desirable but unattainable in this life. For people have to marry outsiders from other villages whom they suspect will try to kill them with sorcery.

At the death of the spouse, the widow or widower must go to their village and suffer deprivation and hard labour for a year. While the body is decorated and exhibited, spouses are blackened and hidden and must never see the skull of their partner. At the end of that year, at the harvest, they are banished and the house of the couple is destroyed. In the case of a man, this means that he will not see his children again.

———✦✦✦———

A note in the Church of England Alternative Service Book:

At Sea. When the [burial] service is said at sea . . . 'the deep' is substituted for 'the ground', and the words 'earth to earth, dust to dust, ashes to ashes' are omitted.

———✦✦✦———

One of the most examined components of the newly fashionable Near-Death-Experience business is lights and tunnels, at least in the West. Other cultures, it seems, experience near death rather differently – the Japanese, for instance, suffer from visions of depressing ponds and gloomy rivers – suggesting the sad conclusion that even in the very throes of death there is no direct experience of reality. Typically, a Westerner travels down a tunnel towards a light or is given a choice between beautiful, golden light and darkness, afterlife being light. This is taken as justification for optimism.

Since classical times an inverted or extinguished torch has been a symbol of death. Our word 'funeral' derives from the Latin term for the torches used at Roman obsequies. They still decorate the doors of vaults in Highgate Cemetery, while the lamps on Italian graves and tombs of the unknown soldier betoken immortality either of life or memory. At Easter, in pre-Reformation times, the sanctuary light was extinguished and relit together with a huge Paschal candle to mark Christ's death and resurrection. We still speak of the dead as having 'snuffed it'.

The Chamula of Mexico see the life of each individual as established in advance by a god who is a mixture of Christ and the Sun.* For each, a candle of different length is lit in the sky. When it burns out, they die.

—◦◦◦—

Leach has argued that religion often plays with different sorts of time by confusing repetitive time, such as the alternation of night and day, and irreversible time, such as life and death.[†] For time always has both continuity and discontinuity hidden in it. By going round and round a bicycle moves forward; either sort of motion can be focused on. By implying an identity of the two, the finitude of human life can be denied and the Valley of the Shadow of Death is converted from a cul-de-sac to a more open-ended structure. Death becomes rebirth and a straight line becomes a circle. Few can attain immortality by association with cyclic time but a recent exception is Martin Luther King who has

*Gossen, 1974:15
[†]Leach, 1961

undergone secular beatification into an American national holiday.

The best known of such cycles is perhaps that of Buddhism where reincarnation is the common lot of Man. Yet here, it might be argued, death is not denied. Rather the acknowledgement of death becomes central to all belief and its contemplation an art form. Visuddhi–Magga thinking contrasts two distinct modes of meditation, *asubha bhavana* (meditation on corruption) and *maranasati* (death-awareness). The former requires meditation on the decaying corpse since attachment to the flesh is the primary source of suffering and delusion through its holding on to the transitory. The latter consists in the realization that death is not a single event but is happening in the body all the time at every level. So that death and decay are seen as the proof of life. It is often assumed that such beliefs bring comfort but Thai Buddhists express as much worry about their fate in future incarnations as Christians once did about Hell. Ecologists may claim to derive consolation from their endless incorporation in the nitrogen and carbon cycles and geneticists speak smugly of the eternity of their DNA, but such sad reductionism has little mass appeal. Everybody wants to go to Heaven but nobody wants to die.

Similar ideas may occur in codes that stress daisy chains of sequence – and so linear time – rather than cycles. But any line that gets long enough becomes a sort of circle. Thus Hamlet to Horatio:

> Alexander died, Alexander was buried, Alexander returneth to dust; the dust is earth; of earth we make loam; and why of that loam whereto he was converted might they not stop a beer barrel?
> Imperious Caesar, dead and turned to clay,
> Might stop a hole to keep the wind away.

Another ploy to defeat time is to alternate from the individual to the collective. In Dowayo ritual, skulls are jumbled up in large jars to mark the transition from individual deceased to collective ancestor. Henceforth, the dead have lost individual identity and

158

their names will not be mentioned again. They have rejoined the 'pool' and are now eligible for reincarnation. This is also the point at which the living reassert their own individuality. The widows sing 'Hitherto we have all lived together. Now I shall fart in my hut and you shall fart in yours.' So flowers are not the only idiom in which to speak of such things.

It is probably this aspect of mortuary ritual that explains anthropologists' obsession with death as evidence for the importance of the collective over the individual. Indeed, Maurice Bloch has suggested that a switch from the individual to the collective in funerary rites is an inevitable part of those societies that see themselves as formed on an unchanging eternal model whose roles are merely temporarily filled by individual incumbents.* Again, the generalization fits where it touches. As we have seen above, dead Sakalava kings are replaced by living replacements whose bodies are taken over by them. They *individually* become eternal.

By translating ritual into general statements about the individual and the collective, thanatologists have already adopted a collective language that has little to do with the particular concerns of those related to the dead. These try to salvage what is useful, reallocate power and responsibility and generally keep the world turning. General statements are the mere fixed points by which they navigate – not the object of the exercise.

Moreover, exactly the opposite argument has been advanced by scholars.† In traditional, face-to-face societies, it is claimed, interactions are so rich and varied that every individual is indeed unique. In modern urban society, life is based upon depersonalized interactions of strangers so that individuals are mere fillers of roles and are usually stripped of their most important functions through enforced retirement long before death. Hence the number of those that attend any person's funeral is smaller and smaller, since they reflect bonds of affection rather than social role. This is carried to its logical extreme in the increasingly

*Bloch, 1982
†Kearl, 1989:84

common discovery of decayed bodies in city tenements years after their deaths. Socially, they had ceased to exist long before they died.

Not that this phenomenon is limited to urban societies. Among some Australian peoples, the old, who are no longer ritually active, on their death are buried without further ceremony, dead to rites.

—⟨ΘΘ⟩—

At some stage the body normally has to be transported, from house to grave, temple, church, whatever. At great public funerals, before the advent of television, the procession of the body was the only part of the ceremony to which the general public would have access. This lends support to the metaphor of death as a form of travel with its concomitant leave-taking.

Around the world, coffins have been frequently built in the form of ships, and nowadays cars. Sometimes these represent folk memories of ancient migrations. Richard Huntington and Peter Metcalf describe how at the climax of a funeral among the Berawan of Borneo a special song is sung that retraces river migrations from the original homeland and so constitutes a route map to Heaven.*

But crossing a river is an obvious way of depicting a clear transition from this world and the nature of the river itself can further enrich the symbolism. Hindus refer to the Vaitarni river that must be crossed by the dead, a formidable obstacle flowing with blood and excrement that recalls the polluting processes of birth.

Traditional Cantonese funerals offer a more sedate journey. A central part of death rites is the writing of the name of the

*Huntington and Metcalf (1980)

deceased on a piece of paper, placing it on a sedan chair, also of paper, and setting fire to both.

English speakers are not alone in referring to the dead as 'departed', 'passed on' etc. The Dogon refer to the ancestors of ordinary mortals as *vageu*, 'those who are far away', these being distinguished from the founding ancestors, the *binu ya*, 'those who went and have come back'. The Lugbara of Uganda see the ancestors as engaged in a slow journey of removal from the living as they are steadily displaced by newly dead juniors. Originally they dwell beneath the compound cluster of their immediate descendants and only gradually, over the years, do they move to the cultivated fields and finally off to the wild bush and oblivion.

Death is more generally full of strange kinds of motion that set it off from life. Among the Indonesian Toraja, life-giving ceremonies involve clockwise rotation, those of death anti-clockwise. Accounts of removal of bodies from around the world mention unusual forms of egress. Corpses are hauled up through chimneys, through holes broken in walls or removed sections of fence. They rush zig-zag i.e. in an unretraceable, unique path, at breakneck speed or creep hesitantly to the grave. Our own hearses require special gearing to allow them to drive sufficiently slowly without stalling; the speeding hearse is a standard feature of film comedy. The Yoruba of Nigeria follow a contrary course. Should someone die in his field, the corpse will be carried slowly back to the house for burial, preceded by a live chicken whose feathers are used to carefully mark the trail at every intersection lest any absent spiritual parts of the deceased become mislaid.

The military have a special death march, with poised and hesitant step, as if bemused by mortality. At President Kennedy's funeral, an empty horse symbolized his role as Commander-in-Chief of the armed forces. So the horse bizarrely signified that he possessed the secret codes that could unleash a nuclear holocaust. In earlier times, such horses might be hobbled to make their tread more appropriate and in Britain the owner's boots would be set in the stirrups backwards.

Before the imposition of the motor hearse, English funerals

were rich in their own variations of motion. Hearses have, of course, been fertile ground for gratuitous motivations, so that Nelson's was modelled after HMS *Victory*. In the nineteenth century, funeral horses were specially trained to prance while mourners trudged. Similarly, the character of pallbearers might be motivated so maids would be borne by maids and bachelors by their contemporaries. This offered scope to nineteenth-century English eccentrics such as Jemmy Hirst of whom it is recorded that he desired fervently to be carried to his rest by maids at a premium of a guinea apiece. Alas, they proved too shy so he had to settle for more accessible widows at two-and-six a time. Among Jews, it is counted the ultimate act of charity to help a complete stranger to the grave so that passers-by may shoulder a coffin for a few steps. Traditional English funeral processions paid no tolls or paid only in pins. The coffin would knock on church walls or crosses *en route* and it might pass over any land and remain immune to prosecution for trespass. Above all, its passage was a unique and one-way journey. The worst form of bad luck resulted from crossing the same bridge twice i.e. making a return journey.*

In 1892, Captain Gallwey, a British administrative official, visited the Kingdom of Benin in West Africa to gain the mark of the king, Oba Ovonramwen, on a treaty.

> ... After the treaty was concluded the King suggested to me that, whilst the Great White Queen was ruler of the seas, he was ruler of the land. Whilst obviously refraining from acquiescing in such a Quixotic suggestion, I was careful not to hurt the King's feelings by protesting, and on that occasion silence was, I am sure, golden.

*Puckle, 1926

Oba Ovonramwen was merely repeating a view of Europeans that went back to the first contacts of the late fifteenth century. In Benin cosmology, the seas were ruled by Olokun, a white-faced god – sometimes a goddess – who sent children and wealth into this world and received them back after death. To travel on the water was to return to Olokun's realm and so to die. It was largely coincidental that a chief shrine to Olokun was in the port of Ughoton, where Europeans first landed and that the first Benin ambassador to a European court was a 'captain of Ughoton'. Europeans failed completely to understand why they were 'fetish' and preceded by courtiers with white rods. They were messengers of the god Olokun.

Five years later, Marines and Niger Coast Protectorate troops stormed Benin in retaliation for the massacre of the diplomatic mission in Benin territory. History had finally displaced myth. But had it? The British deposed the king and took him to Ughoton. There, they put him on a modern steam yacht, the SS *Ivy*, and sent him off into exile over the water. For the British, he had been deposed, mysticism had given way to reality. In his own view, he had died and gone to Olokun's realm.

The notion of death as a journey fits in well with the funeral as a rite of passage, a transition and not just an end. As Arnold van Gennep argued, such rites typically divide into three parts – separation, liminality and re-integration.* Robert Hertz showed that the three phases often mark the fates of both the living survivors and the departed.† The dead must be separated from life and undergo processing to join the community of the dead. The state of the body reflects the state of the soul and, by implication, that of the living survivors. The bereaved must be separated from the deceased and finally reintegrated into the living. But both living and dead undergo a liminal period where they are betwixt and between, 'in passage', and most religions distinguish between the outcast spirit of the newly deceased and the integrated ancestor.

*van Gennep, 1909
†Hertz, 1907

Among the living, this stage is called mourning and marked by all manner of restrictions on permitted activities. Among the dead, it is limbo, a period where they may be confused, unhappy and particularly dangerous to the living.

This approach has become the standard way for anthropologists to see death and comprises almost all the intellectual capital they have to expend on the subject. Curiously, they have seldom noted that the dead and various categories of the living may not all be at the same stage in the process. Thus, the widow may well be still in 'liminality' while everyone else, including the dead, has long since reached 'reincorporation'. So the view that the physical state of the body shows the state of the soul *and* of the living is hard to maintain if these are out of kilter. Moreover, some cultures seem to stress one stage of the process rather than another. Such an analysis shows Western funerals as curiously unbalanced. Stressing as they do the uniqueness of the dead, they deal heavily in separation and liminality but have very little to say about reintegration, leaving the mourners high and dry in their grief and the dead with no place to go.

It is because Westerners associate funerals with the expression of respect, that elements involving sexual licence seem puzzling. Lingering Freudianism encourages us to see sex as what everything else is 'about' but neglects that sex itself is often used as an idiom in which to speak of other things, including death. Sex is a sufficiently flexible symbol to turn up at just about any stage of a rite of passage, a manipulable symbol to die by. It can be repressed or exuberant, ordered or chaotic. It is not then, sex itself but what *aspect* of sex is stressed that is important at a death.

Sexual abstemiousness at death – to us normal – occurs largely in the first two stages of a rite of passage, separation from society and liminality, while the resumption of sexual relations marks a wider return to normal life. While orgiastic sexual activity, cross-dressing and incest project disorder into the sexual domain and may be an expression of being betwixt-and-between, the image of birth or copulation is easily appropriate to any rite of reintegration, the third stage of a rite of passage. So the sexual behaviour of the living, the way they use their bodies, can be just as important for marking the state of the soul as the cadaver itself.

Among the Bara of Madagascar the act by which a dead person's bones join those of its forebears is expressed explicitly in terms of childbirth with the deceased entering the ordered world of the ancestors headfirst like a foetus. 'Here is your grandchild, born here. Do not push him away, even from here.'*

Thonga widows in South Africa, to rid themselves of mourning before returning as marriageable women, must seduce a stranger and, practising coitus interruptus, rub the sexual fluids over themselves, leaving the 'malediction' of death with their unfortunate partner. Dogon widowers of women who have died in childbirth have to have sex with a stranger in order to be cleansed, even if they have to resort to rape. Of course, the fact that we might decide to see this as 'reintegration' rather than 'disorder' derives solely from our selfish urge to protect the cherished 3-stage model.

For both Elizabethans and Hindi speakers, a man's penis after sex 'dies'. As death can be sex, so sex can be death whose clammy grasp is the embrace of love. Victorian fiction is full of the hugging of coffins and swooning maids slipping into the arms of easeful death.

A poem on a tomb in Kensal Green Cemetery illustrates the theme:

> In the dismal night-air dress'd,
> I will creep into her breast,
> Flush her cheek and blanch her skin,
> And feed on the vital fire within.
> Lover, do not trust her eyes,

*Huntington and Metcalf, 1980:116

When they sparkle most she dies;
Mother, do not trust her breath,
Comfort she will breathe in death;

Father, do not strive to save her,
She is mine and I must have her;
The coffin must be her bridal bed,
The winding sheet must wrap her head;
The whisp'ring winds must o'er her sigh,
For soon in the grave the maid must lie;
The worm it will riot on heavenly diet,
When death has deflowered her eye.

Quoted in Morley (1971:43)

On the Indonesian island of Sumba, a rich man may organize his memorial years before he goes and so enjoy the prestige of it directly. You can go to your own funeral. It is similar to our own usage of allowing the terminally ill to cash in their life insurance to have the benefit proleptically of their own demise.

Huge stones are hauled by land and sea over long distances to form a coffin cover that is carved and decorated and reflects the glory of its future occupant. The bones of the previous dead of his group may be placed under it too but it remains *his* grave. The costs are crippling. Hundreds of workers must be mobilized – the more the better – several buffalo must be killed every single day of the journey. Traditionally, it is all done by hand. In anthropological films it still is. But on the cutting room floor are shots of bulldozers, trucks and car-jacks, carefully excised.

The stone leaves the quarry as a bride – a bride incidentally named Wanda – praised for the beauty of her white skin, a daughter of her place of origin.* The purchase of the stone is conducted in the idiom of brideprice and the stone is addressed as by a longing suitor.

By the time it reaches the village, its identity has changed and it is now the other half of such a union, a brave young warrior, and

*Hoskins, 1986

166

its placing over a hollow female element is phrased explicitly in terms of copulation.

—⊸⊱⊶—

Many senior police officers have been victims of ritual murder. In their initiation into freemasonry they play the part of Hiram, the architect of the Temple of Jerusalem, who is slain and raised from the dead. Death itself can, of course, be a way of thinking about other things. It is not only extreme Christians who die to be 'born again'. Those in other religious orders often undergo a similar form of deliberate social death. The robe of a Buddhist monk is the colour of a shroud, the sandals worn are those put on the feet of a corpse. Initiation around the world involves the candidate 'dying' and being reborn. In many African cultures, initiated boys return from their bush camps with new names, doggedly unable to recognize their parents and having to learn how to speak and eat all over again. In medieval Brittany, diagnosed lepers went through a form of attenuated funeral service at which they 'died' and so formally became social outcasts.

—⊸⊱⊶—

Moni Adams has pointed out the importance of fermentation in the processing of natural products in South-East Asia.* Dyes, medicines, fibres and foods are all prepared by fermentation in closed vessels, sometimes with burial, to remove poison or give a more valuable, more potent and stable essence.

Whatever happens to bodies afterwards, South-East Asian funerary procedures usually require them to rot as a first stage. The

*Adams, 1977

167

Thai royal funeral, for example, involves sealing the corpse within vessels for several months. The liquids of decomposition are removed daily. The solid residue is then cremated and reduced to ash that is carried away to be enshrined. The cinders are searched for fragments of burnt bone that become sacred relics. So the funeral fermentation and the treatment of the body are held to involve the same sort of purification as found in humbler processes.

Any technical or natural process that divides into a clear sequence of stages can be used to place death within the larger structure of a life. As well as using the common West African model of the body as a pot, the Dowayos of Cameroon associate each part of a human life history with a particular sort of millet. At marriage a man gives seed millet to a girl's father, after childbirth germinated millet, at death beer is made from malted millet and ancestral spirits are frequently offered the rotted dregs of the beer. The bubbling of fermenting beer in a dead woman's water jar is held to show the presence of her spirit. The English usage – alcoholic spirit, ghostly spirit – goes back to a similar model.

The Dogon of Mali make an identification between alcoholic fermentation and the dead. The disorderly dead who have not yet formally departed to join the ancestors and whose souls wander the village are the cause of fermentation in beer. Beer drinking is reserved for meetings connected with the dead and is especially drunk by old men. It enters into them and disorders their thought and action. Its effect is a warning to the living from the dead to undertake the expensive ceremonies that promote them to ancestorhood.

——✺——

In British churchyards there are crowds of people who – terrifyingly to an African visitor of mine – were buried when, according to their headstones, they 'fell asleep'.

Our word 'cemetery' is from the Greek, meaning 'sleeping place'. There is an inevitable assimilation of death to sleep in traditional Christian belief because of the dogma of the resurrection of the flesh at the Last Trump. To this day we still creep awkwardly around dead bodies with hushed voices and whispers as though they could be 'disturbed'. The need to draw a firm line between sleep and death is marked by 'wakes' where the living sit up around the dead and sleep can be punished by death.

If death is sleep, then the grave is a bed which leads to the custom of burying husband and wife together – but generally only in pairs. Thanatological practice makes no allowance for serial polygamy. A vicar I suggested it to found the suggestion scandalous. 'After all,' he declared, 'they were not all wed one with another *at the same time.*'

If the tomb is sometimes a house, so is the human body. In our own culture, we tend to limit each room to the exercise of one physical function, sitting room, dining room, bathroom etc. The house becomes a map of different physical activities. Rooms are graded in terms of public and private. The further you move from the front door, the more private they become. Most personal of all are bedrooms with all manner of rules governing access and our basic rule that a 'normal' household only contains one sexually mature couple. Undertakers say that part of the increasing urgency of removing the dead from British homes lies in the disappearance of the 'parlour' or 'front room'. This was a special public room of high formality that might not be used except for the reception of guests and suitors. Here, heirlooms, wedding photographs, best china, symbols of family achievement such as the children's educational certificates and sporting trophies would be on show. The possession of such a room was heavily related to notions of family respectability. This, the public 'face' of the house, pointed towards the outside world and was the only correct place for a body to be displayed, with its eyes closed and the curtains drawn. As soon as the corpse left the house the front door would be declared out of bounds.

Among the Alaskan Tlingit, the eight long bones of the body

169

were associated with the eight beams of the house. The back end was the house's 'head'. The door was its mouth. As is frequently the case worldwide, dead bodies could not be removed by any of the normal openings in socially important boundaries, though the mouth of the corpse and the house door had to be fixed open to allow the 'breath' of the deceased to escape. A special hole would be broken in the (back) wall and closed up again to allow removal for cremation. Significantly, birth occurred outside the house at the rear, the child being brought in via the front and cleansed with ash so that in the course of a life a complete cycle was completed

—

In the West, we are told, death is 'meaningless'. We believe that we alone see death in all its brutal factuality. It seems unlikely that we would find any parallels with these metaphorically rich but 'delusionary' rites of other peoples. But wait. Surely it is the very metaphorical nature of our view of death that makes it so problematical for us.

A philosophical tradition going back to the mind/body dichotomy of Descartes encourages us to see the corpse as a defunct machine of which we are the outraged owners. Indeed, we take Descartes' ideas further. He at least thought the soul was located in the pineal gland. We conflate it with the abstract mind so that it may truly be said that in our notion of death we have put Descartes before the hearse.

Machines have long given us new ways of seeing our bodies. Harvey's notions of the circulation of the blood were made possible by the demonstration, a few years before, of new and improved water pumps. Nowadays the machine body may break down unreasonably early, or slowly wear out and become capriciously disfunctional. Up to a point, it can be cannibalized for spares. Parts may be excised and replaced by artificial substitutes lest we be forced to go prematurely to meet our maker. In our model of conspicuous consumption, the throwaway body becomes another problem of disposal best solved by industrial incineration, grinding down or — more ecologically correct — recycling. The idea of a good death largely disappears, being replaced by that of a fair one based on a reasonable amount of use got out of one carefully maintained body. To die young is not just sad, it is unjust, a violation of consumer rights and guarantee. Beyond that, death is failure, no longer a victory of the spirit over the flesh but a triumph of body over mind. At best it can be seen as a significant nod of approval by Nature towards the British tradition of anti-intellectualism. Disease is the first sharp intake of breath and the emphatic shaking of the head of the cosmic mechanic. Small wonder that in Western hospitals death is unspoken and concealed and doctors swiftly bury their mistakes.

Cartesian machine analogies also colonize brain and even mind, once seen by Ryle as 'the ghost in the machine'. In the 1960s the brain was seen as an immensely complex telephone exchange, a thing of networks, since these were at the cutting edge of technology at that time. Then it became a computer as new machines offered new ways of seeing ourselves. So a new theoretical form of immortality has now been invented by science-fiction writers — that of downloading — in which our mind/brain can be copied on to an electronic medium as one would copy a floppy disk to generate consciousness outside the body. Writers will be sucked into their own word-processors and finally become quite literally 'the ghost in the machine'.

While the model of the machine lurks behind Western conceptions of death, as industrial production is the dominant form of late twentieth-century creation, we have another model that celebrates the individual — that of art — that has evolved in tandem to it. This Western category is concerned with innovation by the individual, creativity that converts into fame — another mechanism by which time may be cheated and the individual live on. Classic works, though rooted in the individual, are 'timeless'. They are housed in museums which are instruments for stopping time, like those rooms 'frozen' on the death of their occupants. Their

171

authors are 'immortals' and collectors often try to attach their names to collections of such works or ornament their tombs with them to ensure their own immortality. Hence the howl of outrage when Ryoei Saito, the Japanese businessman who paid £106 million for van Gogh's *Portrait of Dr Gachet*, two Renoirs and a Rodin sculpture, declared that he would have them put *in* his coffin when he died. It was not only a major act of egotism, it was an attempt to make eternal art merely mortal by incorporating it into the processes by which we treat the evanescent human body. The resistance of art to death is marked by the fact that the death of an artist increases the value of his *oeuvre*. It is a wise career move. Should an artwork itself 'die' the effects are even more dramatic. The last time the *Mona Lisa* was stolen, many more people came to the Louvre to see the empty space from which it had been filched than ever came to see the painting itself.

A similar outrage, in reverse, was occasioned by the curator of an exhibition of Australian aborigine paintings. Wishing to be politically correct, he listed the painters by name instead of merely noting their 'tribe' in the usual high-handed ethnographic fashion. This gave huge offence as, unfortunately, some of the artists were recently dead and native usage absolutely forbids the mention of their names.

—◦◦◦—

Jewish mourning traditionally involves the rending of cloth. In many parts of the world, especially Asia, cloths are woven in complete circles and the cutting of textile warps involves literally slicing through time-warps at breaks in the social fabric such as death, headhunting, name-giving. But rending is a ritual act and demands a bureaucratic, ritual definition. 'The garment must be rent near the neck, in the front thereof and it must not be rent crosswise but lengthwise and in the cloth of the garment and not in the seam. In the case of the next of kin, the rent may be basted

172

together after the seven days of mourning, and completely sewed up after thirty days of mourning, but in the case of a father or a mother the rent may be basted together only after 30 days and never sewed up. A woman may baste it together at once.'*

—◦◦◦—

A journalist once summed up Lady Thatcher's wearily conde-scending way of addressing the electorate as 'talking to you as if your dog had just died'. The human sphere is not peopled simply by humans. We have all sorts of diverse relations with animals that enter into the ways we classify and deal with death. There are domesticated animals that have to be 'humanely' killed, wild ani-mals that are ritually slaughtered in a mockery of warfare and ver-min who invade us and are chemically disposed of in ways wildly in contradiction of the Geneva Convention. Then there is that vast category of others, castrated and spayed semi-prisoners termed 'pets', that we treat as human substitutes. Animal rights activists constantly try to shift such boundaries and the moralities they imply.

Animals become honorary humans. Californians arrange sex-encounter groups for frustrated poodles, while in Brighton there was a vicar who for many years conducted dotty and surely heretical services at which they were blessed. The poet Virgil (70–19 BC) is said to have constructed an elaborate mausoleum for a pet fly. Japanese primatologists in Osaka hold Buddhist memor-ial services for laboratory monkeys they have killed to thank them and ask their pardon, and most Japanese hospitals have a shrine for their animal victims.[†] Offerings are made on altars, the first, on one noted occasion, jointly by a chimpanzee and its keeper.

People can overlap with things and animals. Among the Tlingit

*Habenstein and Lamers, 1960:194
[†]Asquith, 1983

of the Alaska, a shared fate of rebirth meant that bones of animals and fish had to be treated with respect, like those of people. Salmon, indeed, were held to be a race like human beings who lived beneath the earth and assumed fish shape once a year, sacrificing themselves to Man's appetites. After death, they returned to the great house and became human again. If any of their bones had not been returned to the water, they would lack limbs, hobble angrily about peg-legged and not return as salmon the following year. Tlingit artists usually emphasise completeness, depicting animals with important internal organs and bones shown as in an X-ray. And objects, such as canoes, that bore such animal crests, required respect too. When they showed signs of wear they were 'cremated', 'mourned' and replaced by others with the same names. Objects were essentially immortal like dead human beings whose spirits were reborn through the children of their group. The phenomenon was noted early in those African rulers who informed disbelieving Western travellers that they were several hundred years old. In their case this was put down to native mendacity.

It can hardly be said that the pampered children of the contemporary West have the same experience of death as other parts of the world and other ages. We confidently expect our children to survive till adulthood, ourselves to live to maturity and old age; the ultimate gift of a pious son is unlikely to be the coffin offered by a filial Chinese to his living parents. In Britain, deaths of pets provide the only contact with mortality for many children and the model by which they understand it in later life. An informal ritual interment in the garden with some vague intimations of eternity or returning to nature is the solution of most parents unless the pet dies at the 'animal hospital'. Animal mortality is normally very unlike human in that nowadays some 80 per cent of human mortality is insitutionalized and, unlike animal death, is normally without benefit of euthanasia. Not surprisingly, it is occasionally argued that we are kinder to our pets at the end than our relatives.

The natural burial movement, whose underlying idea is that you should bury your own, can be seen as an attempt to use the childhood deaths of pets as a model for human disposal. The stress on DIY, making your own coffin, interring it in the garden with a bit of poetry, is like the budgie laid to rest in a cigar box writ large. This is a neat inversion of those syrupy Victorian paintings that depict 'The Burial of Cock Robin' as a crêpe-hung human funeral of high formality, the animals standing around with arm-bands and top hats. In a world where death has been successively theocratized and medicalized, perhaps it is now to be privatized. Yet to describe DIY death in this way is not to denigrate it. It shows that people are unhappy with current death rituals and are looking for a form of death that ties up with their emotional experience of life.

I asked an undertaker once how she had chosen the paintings on the wall of her waiting room. She had tried cheerful pictures of children, she said, but people found them inappropriate. She had tried Victorian heroines drooping under weeping willows but they had upset people and provoked unseemly grief. It was most important, she said, that the works be 'classics' of authenticated artistic value. The remark oddly echoed one made to me by a military man and shows perhaps a deeper class insecurity. 'The British ranker,' he declared roundly, 'is basically a snob. He likes to be sent to his pointless death by a gentleman.'

The most satisfactory pictures had proved to be those depicting the change of the seasons, chocolate-boxy Constables, suggesting that grief was part of the human lot, as winter was part of the cycle of nature. This is not particularly surprising. In modern life, time is increasingly homogenized – you can buy strawberries all the year round, even on an English Sunday. For many, time is not qualitatively different any more, it has lost its rhythms. It is more like just another running meter.

Similarly, the concern of DIY activists with the wrapping of the body – no hardwood coffins, biodegradable fittings, recycled paper containers – echoes exactly their protests at the unnecessarily wasteful wrapping of fish fingers. Death is being reincorporated into cycles of life, no matter how lowly.

British attitudes to animals seem to infect those that live among

175

them. British cities are littered with animal remains. The gravestone of the Prince of Siam's dog is on a Cambridge traffic roundabout. Every year, thousands of tourists take pictures of the towering monument of the Grand Old Duke of York above Pall Mall. But right next to it, shielded by discreet stone walls, is a diminutive headstone dedicated in German to Giro 'a faithful friend', the dog of Ambassador Hoesch, von Ribbentrop's predecessor at the German embassy. Hoesch, a convinced anti-fascist, was extremely popular with the British establishment and was allegedly poisoned 'like a dog' in 1936 by the Nazis in order to remove him without fuss or memorial martyrdom. Part of that popularity was a result of his adoration of Oskar.

And there was also Mampus. His name was a joke, suitable for a British cat of gravitas and quality but really an Indonesian slang word meaning 'kicked the bucket'. In Latin, he would have been 'Requiescat'.

'He's dead,' said the voice on the phone. 'Dion's very upset. What do the English do with dead animals? What's the law?'

'I don't know. Bury them I suppose.'

'We live on the fourth floor. There's no garden. Dion's terribly upset,' she said again.

You couldn't just throw Mampus's body away in a bin, not a cat like that, big and sleek, a great slayer of mice with a purr like thunder. There were people who arranged animal funerals of course, but they were expensive and Indonesians would think I was crazy to suggest such a thing.

'*You* have a garden,' she said.

There was a silence, long and deep. 'Oh all right.'

They stood at the door, his mother's eyes hot and red, eight-year-old Dion's rimmed in black. 'Such fuss,' she said. 'And for a cat.'

Dion fiercely clutched a large box. Surely he could not have carried it all the way? Bacon flavour crisps, it read. That surely was inappropriate. It had always somehow been understood that Mampus was a Muslim. Even his toilet habits seemed to fit that. When he needed to pee he would poke you with his paw and howl and wait to be escorted to the bathroom, there to squat embarrassed in the shower, then howl again until someone washed it away.

I had dug a hole. A first assault upon the flowerbeds had proved hopeless. I couldn't seem to get down more than a few inches so I had gone for a spot in the middle of the grass under the curtain-twitching gaze of neighbourhood watchers. The grass seemed to have an underlay of bricks, which explained why it did not thrive and finally I had taken a pickaxe to it. I had never realized that burial was such a physical process. This was no neat rectangular slit like a surgical incision. It was a wound torn howling in the earth.

Dion was not impressed. 'It should point East.'

'No sacrilege, now,' said his mother. 'It's a cat.' Then in easy contradiction as Dion started to cry. 'You know better than that. No tears at a funeral.'

I looked in the box. There was Mampus, stiff and sneering but wrapped in a cloth covered with fake Islamic calligraphy. It looked like one of the special headscarves Muslim women were supposed to wear at funerals. Dion looked at me pleadingly. His mother didn't know. He had filched it.

'It's all right,' I said, 'he's lying diagonally in the box, so his head *is* to the East. If we change the hole it won't be right.'

I tried to slide the box into the grave but the edges sloped inwards towards the centre so we had to take it out again and Dion and I worked away with pick and shovel. The dance of death had become a wrestling match. There is no sound as awful as the rattle of dirt on a coffin, even a cardboard one, and afterwards we had too much dirt left over. I didn't think they would want to see me jumping up and down on Mampus so that could wait.

There was an embarrassed silence. We had done what we had come to do yet it had not been fixed and defined. 'Do you want to say a prayer?'

The mother was unconvinced. 'I don't think that would be right. Men know these things.'

177

'Do animals have souls?' I asked. Not the moment for ethnography really but I couldn't resist it.

'No,' said the mother. 'Yes,' said Dion at the same moment. She considered. 'Well. You can get *badi* from a dead cat.'

'What's *badi*?' I had never heard of it, but later I gathered it was the word we translate as 'pollution'.

'It's the illness you can get from being in touch with death.'

This was good stuff, a whole D.Phil. thesis here for someone. Dion stood staring down at the heap of earth, looking very small and forlorn as if a spring had broken inside him that would never be repaired.

'A cat is one of God's creatures,' I opined piously. 'Isn't there something in the Koran about cats?'

Dion shook his head. 'No. There are cows and camels but no cats. Mampus,' he whispered but it was impossible to know if that was the cat's name or a conclusion.

9

From the Cradle to the Grave

The more complete one's life is, the more ... one's creative capacities
are fulfilled, the less one fears death ... People are not afraid of death
per se, but of the incompleteness of their lives.

Lisl Marburg Goodman

In much of the world infant mortality remains extremely high.
International agencies keep a sort of top twenty of such figures as
a general measure of relative 'deprivation'. An African tax form I
once filled in asked matter-of-factly:

1. Do you have any children?
2. Are any of them still alive?

Historians such as Lawrence Stone make a curious assumption of
the cost-effectiveness of emotional investment.* They argue that
eighteenth-century British parents can have cared little for their
children because they knew there was a good chance they would
die. The sentimentalisation of the family is therefore a modern
thing. It would be bold to infer from this that parents elsewhere
have scant emotional attachment to their offspring. It is true that
the passing of children makes little disturbance in public life. Seen
from a wider social angle, individual children are relatively unimportant as they have little social identity and have yet, in society's
terms, to attain full personhood. There are no possessions to be

*Stone, 1977

divided, no dependants to reallocate, no marriage debts to close out. This is the old distinction between social and natural death. Formally, it is always assumed, children will be accorded at most a very rudimentary funeral. Up to a point this is so.

Yet few events can be as personally devastating as the loss of a child. It is because they have been cheated of reasonable life that, according to our own notion of death, theirs are more privately mourned than other deaths, even if publicly muted. Elsewhere in the world, once children have become established as belonging among us, elaborate arrangements may have to be made for them to proceed in simulation through all the remaining stages of life to become real people who can officially die in due form. Then, their deaths actually call forth far greater collective effort than those of even the most prominent adults.

> Another feature of Jizo's statue [the god of compassion], whether in temple, in cemetery, or by the roadside, is the number of pebbles in its lap and piled about its base. According to the belief of many of the Japanese Buddhists, when children die their souls go to a place on the Sai-no-kawara, the Buddhist Styx. Here an old hag robs them of their clothes and sets them a task of piling up stones on the bank of the river. At night, the devils come and scatter the piles, so that the work is all undone. Then the children in their discouragement run to Jizo, who hides them in the folds of his wide sleeves and comforts them. Whenever a worshipper on earth lays a pebble on the knees or at the feet of Jizo's image, he helps lighten the toil of one of these children.*

In modern Japan, children's memorials and Jizo statues are big business. Because contraceptive pills are forbidden and there are great financial and social pressures to control childbirth, abortion is widespread. There are said to be over a million performed every year. The process is euphemistically termed *mabiki*, 'thinning out [as of rice seedlings] so that the others grow better'. There is a fear that the aborted foetus may exact vengeance on the mother and

*Carpenter quoted in Habenstein and Lamers, 1960:60

precautions involve special cemeteries for aborted foetuses at which a statue to Jizo may be erected to help these children that never lived. The gravestones stand in serried ranks, far bigger than the foetuses to whom they are dedicated, and very costly both to buy and to maintain. Nowadays, plastic windmills spin endlessly in the wind before them and presents of expensive toys, still in unopened boxes, lie at their feet. They recall that favourite image of Japan, the *kôkeshi* doll, avidly collected by tourists. These are 'cute' babies with papoose-like bodies, no separate arms or legs, angelic emodiments of endearment. But no child ever plays with them. Rather, they are thought to be images made of the victims of deliberate infanticide, smothered or crushed to death, often by their mothers.

> Both among the Ojibway and other Indian tribes it is a very general custom to cut off a lock of hair in remembrance of their deceased children, especially those still at the breast, and wrap it up in paper and gay ribbons. Round it they lay the playthings, amulets and clothes of the little departed. These form a tolerably long and thick parcel, which is fastened up crosswise with strings, and can be carried like a doll.
>
> They give this doll a name signifying 'misery' or 'misfortune', and which may be best translated 'the doll of sorrow'. This lifeless object takes the place of the deceased child. The mourning mother carries it about for a whole year: she places it near her at the fire, and sighs often enough when gazing on it. She also takes it on her excursions and travels, like a living child. The leading idea, so I was told, was that the little, helpless, dead creature, as it did not know how to walk, could not find its way into paradise. The mother could help its soul on the journey by continually carrying about its representation. This they bear about until the spirit of the child has grown sufficiently to be able to help itself along.*

—◦◦◦—

*J. Kohl, 1985:108

The whole village had echoed to the chopping sound since dusk. The Balinese in the group had been upset, fearing bad luck. There are all sorts of restrictions on what a Balinese can do with a blade after dark. We were a mixed bunch, stranded in a bus that had broken down by the roadside in Sulawesi. The villagers had come out of their houses in search of entertainment, offering sympathy and coffee. It was now nearly midnight and chilly. The driver had lit a fire and was unconcernedly reforging some major factory-made component over a log with a rock as hammer. It would have taken two weeks and cost a fortune to get it repaired in a Western garage. The passengers had split up into gossipping groups. A woman was doing a roaring trade in *pa'piong* she had intended to take to town in the morning, tubes of bamboo packed with rice, chicken and spice. You put them straight on a fire and in minutes, when you break open the bamboo, the food is hot and tastes as if freshly cooked.

Bored, I wandered over towards the chopping. It seemed late to be cutting firewood. A group of men were standing around a young tree, taking turns to shin up the trunk and hack at it with machetes, while arguing about what they were doing. A considerable amount had been dug out some ten feet off the ground and wood chips were sprayed all around.

'What are you making?' I asked. 'A bee-hive?'

A man with sawdust in his moustache grinned. 'No. It's a coffin. My sister's baby died.'

Of course. Death could not be dealt with in full daylight. It was classed with things of the dark. I uttered some fumbled words of condolence and apology and was about to slip away. Then he said, 'It was kind of you to come', and I was stuck and could only think to pass round some cigarettes. A woman emerged, covered in black cloth, and sat down in a collapsed heap, sobbing.

'My sister,' the man explained, 'her husband's away working as a sailor.' He worked his jaw tightly. 'I reckon all this is because he went to the smithy while she was pregnant.'

Torajans worry about smithing interfering with human birth

because sex and smithing are seen as too much alike, both involving heat, percussion and transformation. There is a danger they will get tangled up, the metal will be spoiled, the child miscarried. Anyone involved in birth should keep clear of smithing. Like a reproach and a threat, the sound of rock on metal rang out from the bus. I groped around blindly for something to say. What would an Indonesian say?

'Are there other children?'

'Not yet.' He took a deep, slightly shaky breath. 'Lucky it wasn't a boy.'

Damn. *That's* what I should have asked. They brought out a tiny package, wrapped in cloth, gently pushed it into the hole in the tree and tied round the trunk a sort of woven bandage of reed, puffing away on my shop-bought cigarettes.

'I worked in Malaysia,' said the man, tapping his knife against his leg with the sound of metal on wood. 'You know, cutting down the forest. When they bury the birthstring there they plant a coconut over it and it grows with the child. Here we do it the other way round. In a year or two the tree will close up and keep on growing – like a child.' He pointed with his blade and I now saw other patches, like old scars, on other trees.

There was a furious honking and flashing of lights. The driver must have completed his repairs, remounted the piece and wanted to be off. I found I had no idea what to say. But then, in England, I wouldn't have known either. Should I speak to the mother, sitting there, shaken by silent sobs? It seemed rude to ignore her, impertinent to speak. She did not, after all, know me. And what could I possibly say? I was becalmed without a proper gesture. Neither a little bow or a handshake seemed right. But miming quiet embarrassment is an appropriate way of showing respect in Indonesia, so I just hovered. The driver honked again, longer, more insistent. I had now lost my assured seat in the bus and would end up perched for hours on one buttock by the door with a baby being sick on my lap. To my relief, the mother stood up, blew snot on to the ground and went inside. The men got a wave. Handshake and hug for the brother. 'You will soon be an uncle again,' I risked in a whisper. He looked at me surprised. Finally, I had said the right thing.

'You noticed,' he said, grudgingly impressed. 'And in the dark? You must be a married man. Yes, she's pregnant again.'

—◦◦◦—

At least until the mid-eighteenth century, it was common practice in England to give a new born child the same name as a living elder brother or sister. There was little risk of confusion as the chances were that only one of the pair would survive till adulthood.*

Among the Alaskan Tlingit, names were among the most important property redistributed after death, since names are the very stuff of which social identities are constructed. In most non-European languages 'name' translates as 'fame' and 'reputation' too. Similar systems are recorded in New Guinea and South America. Names can be as scarce a resource as food and people may have to queue up for a name and the identity it confers.

Each Tlingit clan owned a fixed stock of names that were constantly recycled through the generations. Each individual had 'birth names' that linked him with a reincarnated ancestor and 'big names' whose allocation had to be marked by the distribution of gifts. Names could be lost, disgraced and abandoned, or transferred as valuables from other clans. It was the names that were seen as the ongoing constituents of the clan, not the people. Individual people were merely holders of names. If there were not enough people to carry all the names, more would be adopted.

—◦◦◦—

*Gittings, 1988:7

184

African masquerades are principally men-only affairs. Yet in the Bissagos Islands of Guinea Bissau, there are festivals where girls dress up in elaborate animal costumes and masks, sport weapons, play drums, dance and undergo complex rites of initiation.

But they are not doing it on their own account. They are doing it for dead boys. Boys who have not gone through the full ritual cycle cannot complete the full journey to the spirit world. They are stranded on the westernmost island of the Bissagos group and dangerous for the living – especially their mothers. Living boys must go through the rites on their own account. From the point of view of the system, however, girls are spares.

The operation begins when the spirit of the dead boy invades the body of a young girl from his group and over the next few years she acts as the substitute of the deceased in an accelerated transit through the different grades of initiation. Often the boy in question was a mere infant. Part of the work of the possessed girl is to give an individuality to the boy, to develop a character with its own little gestures and personality, like an actor.

The boy's mother becomes her adoptive mother but the boy is also considered her husband so that she has to refrain from sexual relations with others. Social scientists at one time used to like to 'explain' such usages in terms of emotional compensation. Through the rites a neglected girl becomes the focus of concern of the whole society, gains its attention and basks in the reflected glory of her spirit husband. Initiation provides a route by which she may later become a priestess, a woman of influence and rise to great prominence. Her extraordinary powers are ascribed to the dead male who possesses her. But it is only through the living girl that the dead boy attains simultaneously both to manhood and marriage and so can pass on smoothly to his proper place in the world of the dead. Any judgement of who has the better of the bargain depends on what you think is 'real'.

In fact, it is not that unusual for the dead to be symbolically promoted through all the grades of life to attain adulthood. The Balinese mark full social maturity by filing the teeth of their children so that they no longer have sharp incisors like animals.

185

Should anyone die before attaining this state, they will undergo the operation after death. Among the Chamba of Nigeria and Cameroon, should a woman die in childbirth and be found to contain a well-formed male foetus, it will be circumcized to enable it to attain reincarnation.

The Nuba of the southern Sudan are unusual, if not unique, in that they practise circumcision *exclusively* on the dead. The explanation for this lies in the fact that males of one group were previously abducted by Arabs and forcibly circumcized. Since Nuba believe that the circumcized and uncircumcized go to different places after death – drawing a line between themselves and their neighbours – they now circumcize all males of that group immediately after death so that they can rejoin their unfortunate, kidnapped forebears.

The Karo Batak of Sumatra are alleged to have gone rather further. Children underwent a sort of marriage after death that was consummated by the dead boy's penis being wrapped in warm bamboo or a banana being inserted in the dead girl's vagina.

In Transylvania it is still the custom to marry an unwed corpse to a living person from the same village who recites the appropriate vows over the coffin. A dead girl is arrayed in a wedding dress and interred with a doll to replace the children she will never have.

Technology does not destroy such practices. It allows even more elaborate ritual processing of large numbers of dead. In America, the Mormons use vast computers to baptize the dead retrospectively and eternalize their data in a nuclear blast-proof shelter. They also seek to embody the future – a sort of Mormon replacement therapy – by urging the faithful to reproduce to provide bodies for spirits caught in pre-existence. Such concerns to subject the dead to due process are not marginal to modern politics as can be seen by the passionate mid-1970s debates in the American Congress on whether to restore American citizenship to Robert E. Lee, the Confederate general, who – one would have thought – was way beyond caring.

186

—⟨ℓℓℓ⟩—

Insults at funerals may be part of a larger 'joking relationship' but there are some dead who are insulted because of the circumstances of their passing, because their deaths are 'bad'.

In Budapest in 1279 a Church Council was held to curb the system whereby victims of murder, falls, fires and collapsing buildings were charged a fine before they were allowed Christian burial. Theirs were deemed bad deaths.

The term 'bad death' confuses several ideas. There are those that are slow and painful, not nice ways to die. In many parts of the world they will be viewed as resulting from human malice, sorcery and witchcraft. Or death may occur at a bad place or time, far from home, making the body irrecoverable. Such dead may give rise to dangerous spirit beings but their power can occasionally be redirected. The Maori converted them into war gods for use against outsiders.

Some people employ a sliding scale of almost actuarial precision – often calibrated along some basic dimension. So the Alaskan Tlingit grade deaths in terms of wet and dry. The worst death is drowning. This involves the loss of the body and so the hope of human reincarnation. The bodies of insignificant slaves, being mere rubbish, were dumped on the beach between high and low tides. Normal bodies were burnt which ensured a place by the fire in the village of the dead. This was pictured as a wet, comfortless place where the unloved shivered and became 'Mossy eyes'. Warriors slain in battle were drier. They turned into the northern lights and their scalps would be dried and kept. Shamans were so dry they could be removed directly via the chimney and be simply placed in a gravehouse without further treatment.

Yet other deaths are bad in that they violate the sense of what is natural: children who die before their parents, those who are struck by lightning or afflicted by leprosy where the flesh rots like a corpse while a person is yet living. Above all, there are women who die in pregnancy or childbirth, life-givers who become death-dealers. While these forms of death may involve the idea of punishment – death in childbirth is caused by adultery, for instance, and death by lightning only affects witches – the badness lies less in the moral state of the victim than in the manner of death itself which is an offence against nature.

It is comparatively unusual for death in childbirth to be regarded as a good death. An exception were the Aztecs because they equated it with a warrior's killing. Death was so dominant that even normal birth was equated with the taking of prisoners for sacrifice. The midwife even emitted war cries.

In West Africa, such deaths are conventionally phrased as involving an offence against the Earth, may involve the mutilation of the body and stop the cycle of life dead in its tracks so that the deceased are excluded from proceeding on to ancestorhood or rebirth. An Asante woman who dies in childbirth is insulted by all the women of the village and dumped on the rubbish heap.

James Fox relates that on the Indonesian island of Roti, the normal dead were formerly buried under the house and their spirits are still held to take up residence within it, in the loft.* Which house you were buried under finally fixed the somewhat fluid kinship links of an individual and increased both the spiritual power of the house and its claims to share in the inheritance. Babies were buried under the entrance ladder in the hope of swift rebirth.

A woman who died in childbirth, a bad death, had to be carried to the grave back to front and became a dangerous spirit in the form of an owl. The Rotinese sought to prevent this by sticking needles in the fingers of her hands and eggs under her armpits to inhibit the growth of her wings.

Similar fears are common in much of South-East Asia. In Malay culture, a mother dead in childbirth becomes the terrible demon *pontianak*, roaming the world in the guise of a beautiful and wan-

*Fox, 1973

188

ton woman, beguiling men and suddenly revealing herself as a hideous, long-nailed harridan who strangles them in her sexual embrace. Among the Iban of Borneo they are *antu koklir* that above all attack the genitals of men. You are warned that when you walk through the forest at night and encounter a beautiful smell you must pretend to be disgusted by it. It could be the perfume of such a spirit beguiling you. Never say anything nice about the smells of the night!

The young man was bent over his computer, scowling intensely at the screen. 'Hang on,' he called over one shoulder. 'I don't really sell the tickets. I'm an archaeologist.'

I was in Rabat – not the one in Morocco – but the homonym in Malta where St Paul was shipwrecked while on his way to Rome for trial. He took advantage of the unscheduled stopover to convert the Roman governor and in doing so gave birth to a tourist industry that is still flourishing. The town is riddled with catacombs, hollowed out of the soft, honeycomb-yellow Maltese rock and legend happily associates several with St Paul.

'The tombs here have nothing to do with St Paul. You appreciate that?'

'Yes. I know. Those are the ones by the church.'

He snorted. 'All hearsay. There's no evidence for that either. I am an archaeologist so I tell only the truth.'

There was nothing for me in that so I let it ride, bought my ticket and went upstairs to the little museum while the archaeologist gathered together other sheep to make a flock worth unlocking the gates for. Biblical imagery is contagious.

It was the best sort of museum, like the schoolboy's shelf of bones and rocks afflicted with gigantism. There were Carthaginian pots, mammoth tusks, lumps of iron ore and a whole room devoted to baroque horrors such as the severed head of John the Baptist, baked in clay, and a depiction of St Paul's shipwreck in cut-out figures set in a deep frame like some prefiguring of television. Then we were called down to the catacombs.

We were an odd bunch. Several Germans, furiously translating for each other, a French family including a dry, aged grandmother who spoke out loudly against Anglo-Saxon linguistic imperialism and a hugely fat Irish woman with tiny weedy husband who tutted her enjoyment of the promised horrors.

'This is *not* a tomb,' our bored guide was saying. 'It used [yawn] to be a tomb but now it is a church. The paintings have just been restored. They were restored all wrong in the nineteenth century so those had to be removed for it to be done properly.' He sounded irritated as if he had been made to do the work himself. 'All the tombs are connected in long tunnels but originally it was not like this. As the doors were built over, so the tunnels were made to replace them [yawn] but the idea you get is completely false . . .'

We crept around, banged our heads, learnt the difference between trough and window burial, took no photographs, touched no bones, abraided no surfaces with our hands. Then, in a narrow tunnel, the Irish woman got stuck. Her husband tried pulling, then pushing, then just danced on the spot, arms dangling, not knowing what to do as she stood embedded in the rock like a fossilized mollusc.

'For the love of . . . Will you not breathe in Bridget? Draw yourself innnn.' He mimed spectacular concavity.

The guide had not noticed. '. . . so there you see the table was removed on which the dead were previously supposed to eat with the living [yawn] and in this painting you see . . .'

The French were trapped the wrong side of the wretched woman and began protesting their deprivation. 'Ah! Zut! Alors! It is because she is pregnant,' observed the old lady.

'I daren't pull meself about,' whined Bridget. 'It's bad for the baby.'

'. . . and here you see the shell, symbol of eternal [yawn] life. I

190

am telling you all this in three minutes though in the thesis it took years of serious archaeological research. So the Communion is supposed to replace the pagan idea of the living eating with the dead...'

'It's your coat, woman. Take off your coat and you'll get through.'

Bridget began executing a sort of grim parody of a stripper's bump-and-grind routine while her husand pulled and poked uselessly at her sleeves. With a final wriggle she at last slipped through and the coat fell to the ground.

'Ah! Zut! Alors!' The French scuttled through in her wake.

'... and as for the smallness of the cavities most people assume [yawn] – quite wrongly – that people were very short at that period. But you see, the dead were buried as babies, drawn up, so that is why everything is so small. This whole place was built for babies and rebirth as babies into the next life. And now [yawn] there is no way out here so we must all go back the way we have come.'

It was a moment before we realized his last comment was a direction to the exit not a statement about mortality.

'Ah non! Zut! Alors!'

—◦◦◦—

Until the abolition of the death penalty for murder in Britain, it was still the practice in the twentieth century for the hanged to be buried in corrosive quicklime in the prison yard without a marker – a procedure that caused difficulties when, as with the Irishman Roger Casement, 'traitors' became 'patriots' and their bodies had to be reconstituted for formal and honourable burial in a now-recognized homeland. A full coffin was always managed somehow, whatever went into it.

Previous centuries had different priorities deriving from the public nature of execution. While those condemned would often

191

wear punctilious mourning dress, youthful miscreants would dress as brides or grooms to complete their earthly course.

It cannot be assumed that life and death are everywhere simply opposed as in our own thinking. Ritual may equate one with another. There is a moment in Maasai ritual where a sacrificial bullock is suffocated with milk, honey and a woman's skirt, normally symbols of life,* and its meat fed to young men so that they may be 'reborn', or promoted, into a new age-class.

More generally, a belief in the reincarnation of the dead encourages the linking of children as much with death as with life. High child mortality rates can be seen as a mark that children are eager to return to the land of the dead. Among the Alaskan Tlingit, children were expected to remember previous existences while they were still infants. Only much later was the shrivelled umbilicus they wore around their necks cut and such recollections discouraged.[†]

Over much of West Africa, there is the belief that certain children are 'ghost children', malicious beings that are born in pain and suffering, inflict anxiety and grief on their parents and then malevolently die, only to get themselves born again. These monstrous children feast on their parents' suffering and sell their tears for huge sums in the land of the dead. If identified in time they will be given names that refer to their ugliness or wickedness to make them unattractive to spirits or smeared with repulsive matter so that the closed circle can be broken. After death, their bodies may be mutilated.

———

It was Margaret's second year reading anthropology. Her specialism was Africa and she was not doing well. Initially, there had been

*Arhem, 1990:226
†Kan, 1989:108

the usual unavoidable problems for any pushy Yoruba girl studying a foreign vision of her own culture. To her it was all about as convincing as Dick Van Dyke doing a cockney accent. But she was fighting back doggedly. At the end of a particularly tedious lecture on kinship and social control she had risen to her feet and shouted thunderously at the terrified lecturer, 'You say all these things about pressure from control of economic resources and witchcraft accusations but I love my mother because she gave me her breasts and for no other reason.'

But her file confirmed that something was wrong – declining marks, undelivered essays, absences. And you only had to look at her face, grey and slack, exuding a sort of hopeless weariness, to come to the same conclusion. We were supposed to be discussing her forthcoming term paper but I was also in the position of being her 'moral tutor'. I had a sort of set speech to introduce the notion to new students. 'You will find your principal problems are from personal relationships, lack of money, shortage of accommodation and pressure of work. Please remember that your moral tutor has the same problems.' From the look of Margaret, she had them all.

At the beginning of each year we were issued with a bottle of 'sympathy sherry' for moral tutees. I gave her a slug.

'It is my soul,' she said.

'Your soul?'

She nodded. 'I had twin children who died.' The Yoruba are supposed to have the highest rate of twin births on the planet. Twins are smaller than solitary births, weaker. Many die. According to Margaret's file she was nineteen years old and unmarried and I was in charge of her moral welfare.

'We had two *ibejis* made for the dead babies, you know, the little carvings? I looked after them, danced with them, fed them. When I came to England, I brought them too. Then I went to this church in Brixton – a Christian church – and met a Nigerian man. He said I was worshipping the Devil. He said I should give him my *ibejis*.'

Big wet tears welled up in her eyes and her mouth squared for

193

crying. 'And now they come to me in my dreams. I know they want to kill me.'

'Have you talked to this man and asked for the carvings back?'

She reached for the bottle and served herself more sherry. 'He laughed and said he had sold them and given the money to the church but –' fiercely gulping sherry, 'I think he kept the money. He will not say where he sold them. I cannot get my babies back. I went to a *babalaawo*, a wise man, he said I must get new carvings but this is England, where can I get *ibejis*?'

Where had she found a *babalaawo* in England? Maybe this was less serious than I thought. 'Look, I read something about *ibejis* only the other day. We can sort this out. Nowadays, you don't have to make a traditional carving. You can take two prints off a single photographic negative or even use a plastic doll, or you could use an English carving. There is a man at the student health centre who is a bit of carver.' His speciality was owls, I recalled, but that was by the way. 'It's going to be all right. Go back to the *babalaawo* and ask him which of these is best.'

Margaret had brightened visibly. 'You're right. Maybe it doesn't have to be Yoruba carvings. Maybe English would do. It would be like having permanent residence.'

I put the sympathy sherry back in the drawer and slid it firmly shut with my foot.

'Now there is the matter of your term paper.'

Her face darkened and became sulky again. 'I have no subject to write about.'

'Oh yes you have. We've just been talking about it.'

At the bottom of the form that recorded such meetings was a very small box marked 'action taken'. In our culture where problems are always medicalized, you normally wrote down 'referred to Health Centre for counselling'. In Margaret's case it was 'for woodcarving'.

Getting Ahead: War, Murder and Capital Punishment

'The body of a dead enemy always smells good'
Charles IX of France (1550–1611)

What shocks in the literature of judicial death are sometimes less the large horrors than the small civilities: a Tlingit woman urging the killers of her son not to bruise the corpse by letting it simply drop to the ground when they had finished stabbing him, Marie Antoinette apologizing to the executioner for treading on his foot on the way to the scaffold, Anne Boleyn excusing the shape of her neck, the prerogative of British aristocrats to be hanged with a silken cord or the condemned man's right to the breakfast of his choice. In Ancient Rome it was apparently considered wicked to execute a virgin. The ethical problem was solved by having her raped by the jailer. Casts of nineteenth-century killers taken in Newgate Prison, after the fact, show the mark of the rope across the throat. In later times, the noose was carefully cushioned with hand-sewn leather to spare the condemned the discomfort of rope-burn. All these seem to show a human gift for going to the very heart of the inessential.

Death by shooting has a nasty totalitarian air to the British way of thinking, the state's use of the army for the repression of its own population, the declaration of a government monopoly on violent death. The British navy on the whole far preferred hanging, an appropriately nautical thing of ropes and knots and yo-heave-hoing. It was comfortably hedged round with beliefs. The still-warm touch of the freshly hanged man's hand could cure disease and was a source of perks for the hangman.

The firing squad is a parody of the hero's death, hopelessly out-numbered, back to the wall, a final imposition of militariness on the cowardly or otherwise unmilitary. In the nineteenth century, convicted traitors were often condemned to be shot in the back. An optional extra was making you dig your own grave first. Yet there is also the concession whereby – in the classic version – one of the killers has a blank cartridge so all may imagine themselves innocent of killing their own. Perhaps this avoidance of actual, individual responsibility lies at the base of the ancient Thai prac-tice of encasing the condemned in a giant rattan football of the sort used in the athletic game of *takraw*. Included in the design, however, were large metal spikes pointing inwards. A game then took place between two elephants which booted the ball back and forth leading to death by football, ripping the victim to shreds through the tangential interplay of disinterested forces far greater than himself.

The most awkward forms of death to cope with are the absurd or ironic, a bishop struck down by lightning as he raises the pro-cessional cross, an old lady bowled over by a large runaway cheese, a man knocked down by an ambulance, since, for us, death *should* be tragic. But then Aristotle's definition of tragedy, a man crushed beneath the statue he had erected in his own glory, is to our ironic sense perilously close to comedy. The piratical walking the plank is another such – a joke gangplank with no land at the end of it, the blindfolded victim prodded with giggles to his doom, death by pratfall.

The Middle Ages devised many forms of nasty public death designed to appal, like the tearing limb from limb of a victim by four powerful horses once his limbs had been 'loosened' with a dagger. Yet there is something unspeakably petty in the French usage of burning the condemned at the stake and then mixing the ashes with those provided by an incinerated copy of the trial pro-ceedings, or – in the case of an author – of his own seditious writings. Perhaps it recalls too closely Kafka's writing machine that cut into the victim's body the law that he had broken.

Yet of all, it is the guillotine that is perhaps the nastiest form of public execution. The device – known as The Maiden – was in use in Scotland long before the French Revolution as another mark of Scottish Continental aspirations. The Germans and Italians used it regularly. Dr Guillotin, a medical man and member of the constituent assembly, took it up and it was formally adopted for the first time in 1792.

Its chief merit was that it was death *by machine*, modern, scientific, egalitarian, almost the first production line, instituted by a committee that tested prototypes on dead bodies and live sheep. Its distinctly modernizing feel recalls the alleged use of dumper trucks in contemporary Saudi Arabia to stone adultresses to death. The guillotine was a great social success. Fashionable ladies did away with crucifixes and wore small guillotines in their ears. The imagination of children too was fired. They made model guillotines and began slaughtering the fauna to such dramatic effect that the authorities were alarmed and had to intervene and confiscate them, the video nasties of their day. At Robespierre's Festival of the Supreme Being in 1794, the powerful filed silently past a guillotine swathed in blue velvet and embroidered with roses, a macabre replacement of the cross or the Virgin Mary.

It admittedly had disadvantages. Even in the eighteenth century it was found excessively wet. The fountain of blood was said to shoot two metres up in the air, inspiring a chronic Lady Macbeth-like haemophobia in its servants. The guillotine operated initially under the name of Louisette or La Petite Louison, derived from the Dr Louis who 'perfected' it. Mysteriously *guillotin* too became feminine, acquiring an 'e' to become *guillotine*. Later it was named Sainte-Guillotine, Dame Guillotine, or La Veuve, 'The Widow'. Why this strange association of the guillotine with femininity? Perhaps the gender of the machine was the start. Perhaps it was pre-Freudian gallows humour based on the thrusting of the victim's head into an orifice before the orgasm of blood or the ineradicable belief in a final pointless erection in the executed. But

197

note, the guillotine is always an *unwed* female, for the liaison is unfailingly brisk and short-lived.

—*ᴗᴗᴗ*—

In a study by the Massachusetts Institute of Technology (MIT) it has been alleged that since at least 1970 an urban American civilian has been at greater risk of violent death than a World War II soldier in action.* This seems to us to represent a damning indictment of Western society. It encourages us to see the modern city as a massively dangerous place where we are at risk of 'unnatural' violence and to contrast it with the security of traditional village life. Yet, according to local explanations around the world, most people are murdered. Some cultures admit the notion of natural death for a small minority of very old people, but in the Third World few people live beyond their forties so that many cultures deny natural death almost entirely. Almost all deaths are attributed to witchcraft and sorcery i.e. deaths through human malice, or slaying by ancestors, or a combination of these.

Cannibalism may be part of this package. The notion of witches who feast on corpses and other human flesh, appears again and again. In Northern India, the dead may have to be symbolically eaten to remove impurity and create fertility, which leads amongst other things to a bowel fixation amongst the priestly class.† In Benares (Baranasi), foul-mouthed and incontinent Aghori ascetics wallow in ritual pollution by claiming literally to eat putrid human flesh from skulls and to sleep with menstruating prostitutes as a way of denying the reality of the everyday distinctions of this world and developing extraordinary spiritual power.‡

William Arens has insisted unconvincingly that all cannibalism is a mere symbolic fiction or a fantasy allegation like that (in the

*Koch, 1985
†Parry, 1985
‡Parry, 1982

present Western view) of witchcraft.* This is why it tends to be made against the people next door, with witnesses always at one remove, a matter of hearsay and common knowledge rather than hard evidence. It is a classic misformulation of the problem – like the old chestnut about why, in some cultures, a man had to marry a woman who was a certain class of relative. It was not so much that, as a freeborn Eurocentric male would see it, you were obliged to marry her. It was more that you had a claim on a valuable woman of that category. So it is with cannibalism. The question is less, 'Did anyone ever do it?' and more 'Why doesn't everyone?' The probable answer is that it is too useful a way of marking humanity off from animals.

The charge that they eat human flesh can be a vivid way of classifying people as animal, as selfish and antisocial, and thereby giving one an excuse for treating them as such. The assertion that people are just 'meat' imposes the same vision on the victims.

But cannibalism can also be used to make deliberate claims to status. In Southern Nigeria as recently as the Biafra war, I have seen warrior groups, operating within an idiom of hunting, who used the ritual consumption of human flesh to mark themselves as 'leopards', fearless shedders of human blood who had moved beyond the boundaries of normality. In the nineteenth century, the Niger Delta Church was so aware of the dangers of encouraging cannibalism that it worried about the introduction of the central cannibalistic rite of Christianity in which worshippers were encouraged to consume the flesh and blood of their saviour. The solution was to substitute a sort of soggy sponge cake known as 'manna'.

Yet there are many well-attested examples of groups where the documented eating of the dead is not only not morally wrong but an act of civic virtue. A rare European use of the model is provided by Abbé Meillet who, during the French Revolution, urged that the flesh of beheaded criminals against the state be delivered to a national butcher's shop so that patriotic citizens might weekly en-

*Arens, 1979

199

gage in a 'Jacobin Eucharist'. His plan was never put into practice, in spite of its logic, insisting that a wrong against the very notion of the collectivity should be expiated by the division of flesh. Perhaps this finds its neatest expression among the Wotjobaluk of Australia where a man who had eloped with an incestuous mate − forbidden flesh − was divided and eaten by the entire group.*

Christianity is not alone in employing a notion such as fathers killing their own sons for cannibal consumption. For the Aztecs, cannibalism and sacrifice were twin faces of death that structured all political, social and cosmic relations. So the world was divided up into allies and victims. Men captured victims in war that were used to feed the cannibal gods and their own blood relatives. The first part of the process of sacrifice was the adoption of the victim as son so that men were seen as giving their own children. Through identification of god and victim in the act of sacrifice, men became gods, suppliers of victims became nobles, outsiders became insiders. Humans fed the gods with human hearts, donned the flayed skins of the victims and ate the flesh left in the temples after sacrifice. Without the flow of blood, the sun would not rise and the sky would collapse, there would be no children. The act echoed a primal sacrifice by the gods in which men had been created from divine blood and the sun from the immolation of godly children. The sun in turn was now to be rejuvenated by human blood made divine in sacrifice.

Sacrifice had its implications in foreign policy in that it militated against either finally subjugating or exterminating the enemies who must supply victims. The blood relations between gods and men were echoed by those between the centre and the periphery of the empire. The victims themselves were not always unwilling since immolation offered guaranteed godhood, a place in the house of the sun and the privilege of accompanying it on its morning course. So death as sacrifice and cannibalism brought men, gods and the cosmos together in a mutually sustaining act that was a model for the state and the whole world.

*Levi-Strauss, 1962:105

—☙—

'So,' Wed said, 'to sum up: English children are being encouraged to enjoy the public torture, burning alive and death of someone whose principal fault was that he had the wrong religion?' A Muslim Minang visitor from Sumatra interprets Guy Fawkes Night.

Behind us, the municipal bonfire of an otherwise politically correct local authority blazed, penned in on common land, the flames licking up in frustrated leftist reflection in the windows of the burghers' Georgian façades.

'Well . . .' I began. Surely I hadn't said anything like that? 'That's taking a very negative view of it. I'm sure that's not how the children see it.' It was an unfortunate moment for the fire to reach the guy perched atop the piled-up wooden pallets. 'Burn baby, burn,' screamed a small boy in ecstasy.

'An American locution,' I explained hastily. 'Must have got that from television. You might want to see Bonfire Night as more a celebration of fire itself. What do you call fireworks? Ah yes, *bunga api*, 'fire flowers'. There you are, then. The power and beauty of fire. A failed historical explosion tamed to beautiful fire flowers. Swords beaten to ploughshares. There are,' I hinted darkly, 'folk-loristic precedents.'

Wed shook his head. 'Exteriorization and demonization of the Other. With the religious terrorism still going on in Ireland, it is all so clear. What is the Bon in Bonfire?'

'Er . . . supposed to be from bonefires, the burning of bones. But that's not the point . . .'

'Look,' said the child's mother, pointing. 'Look at all his hair going up and now his arms are dropping off. There they go!'

The child wriggled and squealed in a swoon of delight. 'Whee! His head! His head!' The head was a slumped blazing ball of knotted rags stuffed into one leg of a pair of old crotchless tights, facial features crudely lipsticked. As we watched, it detached itself and rolled over slowly in a flare of fresh flame as the face melted. The crowd cheered.

'He's dead,' said the little child with grim satisfaction. 'Off with his head! Off with his head!'

'An expression from a classic children's book,' I explained swiftly to Wed. 'Good that children still read the stuff. Not, of course, to be taken literally. We no longer have capital punishment.'

'I read somewhere the fireworks all have names,' Wed frowned. 'Roman candle, Catherine wheel?'

'Oh something to do with the burning of martyrs, but...'

The child had now launched into a stiff-legged imitation of Frankenstein's monster. 'I am the ghost of Guy Fawkes,' he monotoned and grappled with his giggling sister. They collapsed squealing on top of each other. Wed was taking it all in. I could imagine him going back to Padang and delivering a well-turned, slightly appalled lecture on sex, politics and death in English ritual and childhood.

'We must be off,' I urged. 'We ought to drop in round the corner since they invited us. They will have done food, cooked, as you know, on the bonfire, and warm wine.'

'Cooked on the fire?' said Wed. 'You mean like the body?' And warm wine – like blood?'

The child was now trying to pull the head off his sister's doll as she screamed and clawed at his legs and punched at undescended, therefore, impervious, testicles. 'My baby! I want my baby!'

'You little bleeders!' screeched the mother, finally snapping. 'Wait till I get you home. Your dad's gonna kill you.'

I really had to get Wed out of there fast.

———∽∾∽———

Manet's well-known final version of *The Execution of Maximilian* followed numerous earlier drafts. Banned from exhibition by the French authorities in 1869, it was held to be too morally ambiguous since the uniforms recalled those of the French military and might contain a seditious political message – a French political puppet, imposed on the Mexican people, being shot by his own side. His empathy for the Indians was always denied by his looks, that of a blatant outsider, blond, beef-fed and blue-eyed. In pathetic attempts to fix Manet's own political position, critics have been reduced to discussing whether Maximilian's sombrero evokes a halo.

The world of art – like that of death – is full of gratuitous motivations that can only perilously be read as the attitude of the artist. I recall once sitting through an assiduously modern piano work where the artist disdained the normal approach to a Bechstein grand in favour of crawling under the lid and hitting the wires with a book. Only when he emerged from his due of rapturous applause was it revealed that the book was the Penguin *Dictionary of Music*.

In the painting, the moment of the courteous last cheroot is past. In later years, its ash would have been gathered, like that of Che Guevara's which ended up in a plastic bubble attached to the handle of a CIA man's pistol. But taste in those days was no better than it is now and the Emperor's clothes would later be exhibited, bullet holes and all.

The NCO on the right is preparing the *coup de grâce*, two of which were actually needed to finish Maximilian off. After his death the body was stuffed. Since the Mexican embalmer had nothing in his stock of glass eyes to match the Emperor's piercing blue gaze, he replaced the blue with brown. The foreign emperor had finally been Mexicanised.

—⟨ΘΘΘ⟩—

In traditional Fiji, as studied by Marshall Sahlins, death and canni-balism were central aspects of a local economy of political power.* A local myth ties together the arrival of a handsome stranger with the end of incest and the eating of one's own people. Henceforth, chiefs will be of foreign stock but other men, given in return for wives, will be eaten. The principle was articulated as the swapping of 'raw women for cooked men', a neat linkage of two aspects of exchange.

In Fiji, victims were acquired in war, often through foreign allies linked by marriage i.e. receivers of 'raw women' who must return 'cooked men' for eating. The ruler himself, likewise of immigrant stock, had received women from locals and must also give back human flesh to them. In various rituals, the chief is asso-ciated with the victims or the ultimate consumer, the god of war. Most rulers would end up themselves being assassinated and consumed.

Boys were encouraged in warlike activities. Human flesh would be rubbed on their lips. Boys would be encouraged to abuse the bodies of dead enemies or kill and mutilate the wounded. The heads and sex organs of enemies would be hung in the trees where they increased the fertility of the land and people. A man who had never beaten an enemy to death would spend the afterlife beating human excrement with his club while successful killers received titles and honours and orgiastic sexual gratification in this. Massacres of three hundred people or more sometimes occurred if a large village was taken by an enemy.

Social distinctions were observed in the distribution of flesh. Choicest cuts, hearts, thighs and upper arms, went to chiefs and priests. Hands, heads and feet went to the lesser warriors. Scraps went to the boys. Women were not supposed to eat human flesh at all since, in the Fijian view, they were sexually the 'consumed' not the 'consumers'.

*Sahlins, 1983

In nineteenth-century London children could earn a living as gleaners of dog excrement, used in the softening of fine leather gloves for the gentry. The gentry were not shy to thrust their hands into such material. Processed animal matter is quite different from the 'raw' stuff of which it is made. A chilling Nazi term was the word *Menschenmaterial*, 'human matter', with its suggestion that certain people were an emotionally neutral resource to be applied, processed and exploited as if inert. Its logical conclusion was the use of human skin to cover books and lampshades. Nowadays, we are understandably touchy on the issue, easily shocked by other cultures' use of human remains. The ownership of 'human matter' has become a political issue, with museums around the world forced to yield up their stocks of American Indian and Australian Aboriginal bones for 'decent' disposal. Native peoples see them as trophies from an imperial past, rifled from tombs or even the product of deliberate murder to provide 'specimens'. Westerners, having lost their epistemological nerve, invoke the objective claims of a discredited 'science', a value-free right to know. But post-modernism and native rights stand together in their determination that ownership is all about power. Ironically, it is sometimes Western Christian influence that has taught that respect for the dead is a part of respect for the living. So 'specimens' are nowadays returned to the soil as 'relics' even by peoples who traditionally set no store by the ultimate fate of bones and regarded them as relatively inert matter.

In the process, identities are doubtless often reassigned. An American archaeologist once told me that he was excavating an 'old' Methodist site on the East Coast that included a graveyard over older Indian graves.

'It's sometimes difficult to work out who's who and you can't spare the time to untangle them all. The last thing you want in your store these days are human remains, so you just rebury almost everyone as Native American. They make more fuss than the Methodists, anyway. You've got to remember a few years back some Inuit announced they were going to come to New York and dig up a Caucasian graveyard just like archaeologists had done to theirs. Not a damned thing we could think of to say.'

On 20 January 1770, Captain Cook noted an encounter with the natives of New Zealand. 'Some of the natives brought alongside in one of their canoes four of the heads of the men they had lately kill'd. Both the Hairy scalps and skin of the faces were on: Mr. Banks bought one of the four, but they would not part with any of the other on any account whatever . . .' The price paid was 'a pair of old Drawers of very white linnen.' So Maori preserved heads were introduced to Europeans, as European preserved modesty was introduced to the Maoris.

To Western notions of the body, headhunting has long been a mark of savagery. Like cannibalism, it was often automatically assumed to be part of the customs of others to whom one felt superior. There is a possibly apocryphal story that in Cameroon at the end of the nineteenth century, when a German envoy died his escort determined to preserve his body from such heathen violation. This solution was to cut off the envoy's head and take it back to Berlin. The local populace disinterred the body out of curiosity, discovered that he had been beheaded by his own men and were appalled at such an act of German savagery. It became firmly established in the minds of both sides that the others were headhunters, probably cannibals and beyond the limits of civilized behaviour. It is still firmly believed in many Cameroonian villages that tins of corned beef contain cooked human flesh.

A similar sort of process seems to have been at work in New Zealand. Preserved heads, *mokomokai*, were primarily casualties of war both of enemies and kinsmen. The heads of foes were carried home to be insulted and derided. The heads of kinsmen were aids to mourning and remembrance of prowess but an important element in the removal of heads was the desire to prevent others mistreating ones' own. A Maori tale tells of a man, hard-pressed in battle, urging his brother to lop off his head and make off with it to prevent it falling into enemy hands.

Particularly sought-after were the tattooed heads of chiefs, so deeply worked as to be almost carved, with beautiful curvilinear patterns. Such heads, steamed, smoked and dried, rapidly became collectable by Europeans as exotic souvenirs, thrilling evidence of the wild savagery of foreign parts and primitive peoples. As a result, there are stories of slaves or prisoners being forcibly tattooed so that their heads could then be cut off and sold to Europeans. Such heads now figure largely in the debate about the ownership of skeletal remains and are used as proof of the savagery of Europeans to native peoples.

The Cameroonian and Maori cases show that there is no reason to believe the category of headhunting is internally coherent. The ritual treatment of parts of the bodies of enemies may have a similar basis regardless of the part involved. On the other hand, removal of heads may be interpreted quite differently.

———————

In the West, life and death are strongly opposed. Often 'life' goes with 'female', 'death' with 'male'. Death is morally problematic, birth is not. But elsewhere life- and death-giving may not be opposed but in parallel. Part of our difficulty in dealing with the contempt other cultures heap upon women who die in childbirth stems from their idea that, even where childbirth is a good thing, it still involves bloodshed and may be regarded as strongly polluting. We have far less difficulty in accepting the intensely polluted state of, say, a Yanomami warrior who has killed an enemy in battle, an act of which all will be inordinately proud but that we now find ambivalent. But pollution and exemplary morality can co-exist quite happily.

The recent furore concerning females in the military has gone through a predictable cycle. For a long time they had been permitted at the 'caring' end of combat, as nurses and in catering and clerking, but they were not allowed to partake in death-dealing. The price they have paid for tolerance is bizarre male-style uniforms, suppression of 'feminine' traits such as long hair and make-up, dismissal for pregnancy, and assumptions about their sexuality.

By a curious inversion, in the West, death-dealing is held to en-hance the potency of males that engage in it, to make them more virile, more 'masculine'. Typically, Western man is more concerned with virility than fertility. This escalation of maleness is not true of killing in the human domain alone. The phenomenon is familiar amongst American men in the form of trophy hunting and fish-ing.

Western armies function as institutions for increasing virility and the same arguments that were once advanced to show the absolute impossibility of having females as regular troops are now advanced against male homosexuals. Other armies have structured a different relationship between death-dealing and gender. The Azande of Zaire, until the colonial period, encouraged exclusive homosexuality in the army élite while the Greeks often saw active homosexuality as an excess of masculinity and so eminently suited to death-dealers.*

The Iban of Borneo associate the male pursuit of headhunting with a more general fertility. Only when a boy had taken a head was he marriageable, a proper man. Nowadays this shedding of blood may be that of the man himself since tattooing has become a touchstone of masculinity. Dreaming of felling trees for rice-growing was an omen of successful headhunting – the two activities were carried out, exclusively by men, at the same time of the year.

The point about headhunting in South-East Asia is that it is a life-giving death. It makes the rice grow, the women have more children, cures the sick, makes children strong. The precise mech-anism by which this works has occasioned much bickering among anthropologists but seems unproblematic to the Iban themselves.

Derek Freeman shows how ceremonial rice, *nasi pun,* is grown by strict analogy with headhunting.† An incantation equates the sprouting of the many heads of rice with the enemies of the Iban. Both must be reaped and dried for life to flourish. The human

*Dover, 1978:164
†Freeman, 1970

heads are described as being treated as babies that cry. They are nursed by female spirits but continue to cry. It is only when transvestite priests, *manang bali*, take them that they laugh. These reconcile male and female, life and death, to release fertility.

—⁓—

In 1231, the pious Elisabeth of Thuringia died at the tender age of twenty-three. She had spent her life in selfless caring for the diseased and suffering. Her piety and self-sacrifice made her an obvious candidate for sainthood. Before her body was even cold, the citizens of Marburg, in frantic devotion, cut off her hair and nails and sliced off her fingers, ears and nipples. Finally, they stole her shroud.* When the eleventh-century hermit St Romuald spoke of leaving his Umbrian village, the citizens, fearful of losing the relics to be derived from his body after his death, conspired to murder him.

The body, normally an object of dread and pollution in medieval Europe, could be converted into a powerful source of curative and protective miracles. One did not even have to be human. In South-Eastern France for hundreds of years there flourished the cult of a holy greyhound.† Relics offer an example of a feat of reclassification in which human remains that offer irrefutable proof of death are held to be the key to life. The whole of Christianity, after all, functions beneath the symbol of the cross, a primitive instrument of torture transmuted into a mark of immortality. Even the most absurd and polluting parts and products of the body are deemed *relatively* holy when compared to the normal human condition and indeed gain strength from the obviousness of their reversal in value. Thus, just as purifying properties are attributed to the urine of holy cows in India, the miracle-working prepuce of Christ is to be found

*Muensterberger, 1994:70
†Schmitt, 1988

not only in the Church of San Giovanni in Laterno but also in Charroux, Puy and Coulombe in France, in Santiago de Compostela, and even in Hildesheim and Antwerp. Despite its impeccably Protestant credentials, the Church of England retains ancient altars that incorporate the bones of saints.

Such was the creativity of holy relics that they could be infinitely subdivided and each part would retain full power. Should there be doubt as to the authenticity of competing remains, they could be laid together and the false would be symbolically transformed into the true so that the huge amount of wood claimed to be from the true cross was quite irrelevant to claims of its authenticity. The same quality, it may be noted, characterizes the lucky red underpants of the racing driver James Hunt. It is alleged that whenever they wore out a new pair could be substituted as long as a small patch of the old pair was sewn on to them, and so on through whole generations of undergarments.

Reclassification depended in theory on a deliberate act of elevation, after which the relics might be bought, given or stolen without impugning their status as moral instruments of divine will.* Relics were one of the principal constituents of the booty brought back by the Fourth Crusade after it sacked Byzantium in 1204.

This treatment of the body by reclassification is not unlike that of other objects in the West that normally have to pass through a stage of being 'junk', before attaining the elevated status of valuable antiques.†

The sweat of Elvis Presley, distilled from the woodshavings scattered over the floor of his concert venues, can be bought in plastic phials.‡ Joni Mabe, who has made a career of exhibiting Elvis Presley memorabilia, owns a wart said to have been cut from the wrist of 'the King'. It was the centrepiece of her Los Angeles exhibition, together with an Elvis toenail.

---

*Geary, 1988
†Thompson, 1976
‡Marcus, 1992

Her pop-art collage commemorating the first anniversary of Elvis's death is a make-believe fan letter surrounded by photographs of herself, bare-breasted and in intimate contact with an effigy of Elvis. The letter says in part: 'I could have saved you, Elvis. We could have found happiness together at Graceland. I know that I could have put your broken self back together. It's as if you could have discovered that sex and religion could be brought together in your feelings for me. I worship you . . . I no longer know the difference between fact and fantasy. Elvis, I have a confession to make. I'm carrying your child. The last Elvis imitator I fucked was carrying your sacred seed. Please send money. Enclosed are photographs of myself and the earthly messenger you sent. Love sick for you baby . . . Joni Mabe.'*

I met Joni Mabe, very briefly, in Los Angeles. She was taking down her exhibition in Ernie Wolfe's gallery. The walls swarmed with paintings, collages, objects. The wart was there. I was offered a biscuit that had some special Elvis significance. She was dressed in a kind of cowgirl outfit and spoke with the sort of Deep South accent that twangs like a broken guitar string. It had been a long day with the press and other media. They had had a lot of fun with her, doing those pseudo-serious reports they make about people who believe in UFOs. Yet beneath it you wondered who was fooling whom. After all, they were making fun, while she was making a good living. Joni was telling a story about a pushy radio reporter who shoved a microphone in her face and demanded, 'Sum up the most important thing about Elvis in one word.'

'Way...ull' said Joni, 'he's . . .'

'One word!' snapped the reporter.

'Dayud?' offered Joni.

—⟨ɷɷ⟩—

*Windsor, 1994:58

211

'I would ask you not to touch anything . . .' begins John Ross, curator of the Crime Museum at New Scotland Yard. Standard curator's spiel. A million clammy hands a year can do a lot of damage. But this is no standard museum.

'. . . many of the objects are still contaminated with blood, organic remains or powerful poisons. Some of the weapons are dangerous.' He picks up a ballpoint pen and casually presses the top. A lethal blade shoots out. Everyone jumps.

The museum is basically for training and not open to the public. In a case by the wall are real drugs. That's a proper IRA bomb. I've talked my way in with the aid of curatorial solidarity. It's part of the Met's official guided tour for foreign colleagues but even police officers can wait years to get in. John Ross is a big man with the unexpectedly fastidious gestures that big men sometimes have. You can imagine him standing four-square in a doorway, holding back a baying mob by his sheer ability to embody the law. He has that police habit of standing too close to you, intimidating without uttered threat.

He leads us round. It's a modern plate-glass building but here they've re-created a room from the Scotland Yard we all imagined in childhood, installing a fireplace and a window as if the line between the containing museum and the contained had slipped. In his *The Decline of the English Murder*, George Orwell bemoans the passing of the classic crime – domestic, involving terrible evil in the service of preserving respectability. Here you see what he meant. All the great classics are on show, cheek by jowl, oddly ordinary. Here are the famous German silver fillings that identified a victim in the Christie murders. There is a human vertebra from his garden with roots still embedded in it. They worked out how long the roots would take to grow to fix the time of death. Over there is Dennis Nilsen's bathtub in which he would wash his strangled victims before dressing them and sitting them in a chair so he could go to work and have someone to come home to in the evening. On the cooker stands the big pot in which he boiled the flesh down to sludge before flushing it away. He used it once to cook a Christmas curry for his workmates. The women make

212

faces, but at the filth baked on to the top of the cooker, not the killings.

There are relics from bomb attacks, a Household Cavalry helmet nearly sliced in two. 'You remember the bomb that went off in 1982, eleven killed, some young soldiers on horses just out of their teens? That was the helmet of one of them. The bomb was packed with nails.' He indicates the trajectory that tore into the victim's head. We all go quiet, picturing tearing metal and flesh. 'The Commanding Officer got hundreds of letters a week – almost all of them asking about the horses. How many remember the name of the horse that was wounded?' Most of us do. 'Sefton,' we mumble in shame. 'And the men?' No one.

'Ruth Ellis? The last woman to be hanged? That's the gun.' John lays out the bare bones of the case, flensed like a cadaver, spread like a specimen. 'It seems heartless,' he muses. 'Nowadays they would have gone right for the fact of her recent miscarriage. In those days . . . You can't say they were wrong. It made sense in the world they lived in. In years to come they'll say the same about us.' Relativism, the last refuge of the morally insecure and the anthropologist.

Someone asks about two sliced-off arms, severed at the elbows, waving in a jar like pondweed. He hesitates, starts defensively. 'Policemen have a funny sense of humour. If a colleague's nice to you you think "I've got a deadly disease and he knows and I don't yet." It's not cruel. You see horrible things. If you didn't laugh you'd go round the bend. You see the same with doctors and nurses. It's a defence mechanism.' He nods levelly at the arms. The palms are uppermost, spread in a theatrical gesture of innocence.

'We heard that a suspect had died in Germany so we sent off asking for prints. That's what they sent us – just like that – in a parcel.'

'Armless,' quips someone.

Everyone laughs. He looks round, wonders about the women. Dare he risk it in a politically correct age? 'Lucky we didn't ask for a sperm sample,' he observes naughtily. Over his shoulder I see Jack the Ripper, police photos of all the victims, somehow even more grisly in sepia tones. We look at samples of human flesh set in squares of plastic like holiday souvenirs to be used as desk paper-weights. 'In the old days,' says John, 'juries were less squeamish. Nowadays most things are photographed and judges decide what they can see. In the old days, you just plonked it on a dinner plate and passed it round.'

Stacked against the wall are the paraphernalia from a Victorian whorehouse, a frame with straps, whips, strict governess boots, a Biggles hat. This is the black comedy section. John gamely demonstrates the whipping frame. 'Don't ask why the straps are all adjusted to fit me.' Then his voice drops. 'Sex, violence and death,' he sighs. 'For a lot who ended up here, they are two faces of the same thing. Ask your fancy psychiatrists. There are killers who can only come when the victim dies.'

In one corner, arranged as if on a hall hat stand, are ropes from the last executions. We are reminded that the death penalty is still on the books for things like high treason and arson in a naval dockyard.

'Until very recently,' John confides, 'they still had a gallows in Pentonville. They had to grease it and test it regularly.' He delivers a talk about capital punishment, cool, factual, the words dropping like counterweights. 'A good hangman can go from the accused entering the room to death in seven seconds.' If he got the weights wrong, I recalled, a bad hangman could pull your head clean off. 'It may seem barbaric but it's kinder than gas or the chair – if you go for capital punishment that is.'

The ropes are not what you expect, no Clint Eastwood swirls. One end of the rope ends in a metal loop and the other is simply fed through it. Cheating really. The loop goes under the chin to snap back the neck. By the door are two skulls. The first was crucial evidence in a 1950's murder trial, a clear victim of violent death in a case where the body had been dismembered and scattered from a 'plane. Many years later, when forensic techniques had made huge strides, it was found to have nothing to do with the case. 'That lump on the back,' says John, 'is a noddle – that's the technical term. No one has had one like that for a thousand years. It's an Anglo-Saxon skull. But he *was* acquitted.'

Next to it is a half skull set in silver, nicely patinated, key exhibit in a real-live Victorian melodrama. A serving wench is wronged by the son of the house, then driven away pregnant as a fallen woman. Forced to work on the streets, years later she becomes the madam of a brothel. One day who should walk in but her ex-lover. She kills him, cuts off his head and has the skull set in silver. Every night she drinks wine out of it. It makes the taste sweeter. A death-bed confession is, of course, part of the story.

East Timor was completely normal. It was the late summer of 1991, fifteen years or more since the Indonesian army had 'integrated' East Timor into the rest of the country. There was no doubt that terrible things had happened. There had been pitched battles and quiet, insidious kidnappings, a famine and forced resettlement. A third of the population had simply disappeared without trace. Yet, it was insisted, everything was normal. A special visa? No, no. Tim-Tim was just another peaceful province of Indonesia. Anyone could go there.

The bullet holes in the governor's palace overlooking the sea had been filled and painted over. Curiously, the public relations value of this was compromised by the rusting landing-craft that lay shot-up and beached a few hundred yards further on. The oddest thing was the silence at night. Normally Indonesian towns rage with life till the early morning. Here, in Dili, everything closed after dark. The Portuguese businesses had become Chinese businesses but most were shut.

I was travelling with Billy, my Timorese guide from the other side of the old border. I was lucky to have him, older, more serious and dependable than the others, something of an expert in the cloths I was buying for a museum but with a wicked sense of humour. When we arrived anywhere and could not find good cloths, he would grin and tie one round my neck and make me walk three times round the bus station. People would come up to ask about this weird Westerner and he would start talking about cloths. Before long we would have found someone who was a weaver and end up in their house. As we rode around on the buses, you would see troops out on patrol, checking the gulleys by the roadside. An armed soldier sat at the back of each bus, a rifle, bevelled with use, balanced on his knee.

We arrived at Baucau, a splendid old Portuguese town that formerly tumbled in colonial whitewash down the hillside to an azure sea. They had let it go a bit since and signs of ruin were everywhere. The hotel, they regretted, was closed. It had become an officers' club. In the media later there would be all sorts of allegations about the activities in the cellars of that club.

Billy and I were stranded. There was no bus out that day and nowhere to stay. But Indonesians are friendly people. A Javanese officer came up, asked us a few questions and delivered us to the doors of the barracks. 'You'd better stay here for the night,' he said as if it were the most natural thing in the world.

They fed us bad rice with elaborate politeness and put us in a hut with Buginese troops. Muslims from Sulawesi. It was a new building with windows high up. 'To stop grenades,' one of them grinned. We slept on mattresses on the floor, guns stacked in the middle, Billy and me up one end.

Their shoulder flashes read 'Hasnuddin Brigade', named after the Buginese national hero. I had been to their hometown, Ujung Pandang. We played 'Have you been...? Do you know...?' till late. Quite often I had and did. The Buginese are supposed to have become our English 'bogeymen' but these were sweet-tempered, generous souls. We fell asleep in a wash of warm hospitality.

I woke to a strange sound. There was moonlight streaming through the high windows and gleaming on the guns. Billy was awake too. It was one of the soldiers crying. I don't know what happens in the British army if you burst into tears in the middle of the night. His comrades gathered round making soothing noises.

Several men patted and hugged their friend. Finally one took his head on his knees and stroked his hair to still his sobs. He looked at me and sighed. 'This is all your fault.'

'My fault?'

'Yes. You talked about Ujung Pandang, and it made him home-sick. Yesterday he got a letter from his wife with a picture of his daughter whom he's never seen.' He bent over and whispered in his friend's ear. The man snuffled, dug blindly under the cylindrical pillow and waved a photo of a little girl in a flouncy, hillbilly dress.

'Wah,' I said. 'Isn't she pretty?' though I couldn't really see.

'Yes,' the man began to snuffle again even more loudly. His friend glared at me. I wasn't helping.

Billy and I left the next morning: friendly handshakes all round, a grinning hug from the man who had cried. The sun was shining. Grief had been a terror of the night. I went away impressed at the compassion and emotional innocence of it all, the fact that it was all right to miss your children and cry, that you didn't have to be brutally macho in the army.

A couple of months later, I saw them again on television. They were shooting students, many hardly more than children. I was aghast. I knew these people, and would have recommended any for their decency and kindness. It seemed to call into question all the judgements I had ever made about any people. Could it be them? I must be wrong. Searching the press reports yielded little. The words 'Indonesian' and 'Javanese' were thrown around like synonyms. I watched the tape again. You couldn't see the shoulder flashes. You couldn't really see *anything*. One face, distorted by fear and hate in the heat and dust and flying bullets, looked much like another. You couldn't be sure. Was it them?

I asked an Indonesian friend about it. He was unsympathetic. 'The Tim-Tim people are terrorists,' he said righteously. 'They kill our men. Wouldn't you do the same? *Don't* you do the same in Ireland?'

'Er . . . well. It's complicated. The students would be out on the streets protesting if something like this happened.'

217

'Oh, we did that in Bandung.'

I was surprised. 'You demonstrated against the government? How did they react?'

'No,' he shook his head annoyed at my denseness. 'Not against the government, against the Chinese.' He saw my puzzlement, sighed and explained as though to a simpleton, chopping up each sentence with a hand gesture. 'The Chinese control business but they aren't trusted.' Chop. 'We don't allow them to join the army so they don't get shot like our own people.' Chop. 'So when there's an incident like this it's our people who get hurt.' Chop. 'So then the students go out and hit some Chinese.' Hands cymballed together. 'Look,' he dropped into snappy American. 'Sometimes times are tough. People are getting killed. When there's death around and the shit hits the fan, a guy who ends up with just egg on his face is pretty damn lucky.'

In Memoriam

'Life is a gamble at terrible odds – if it was a bet you wouldn't take it.'
Tom Stoppard, *Rosencrantz and Guildenstern are Dead*, 1967

The Agni of the Ivory Coast have a theory about the randomness of death:

> Originally, Death was good and only struck down the old and frail. God did not waste life and had commanded Death, 'Strike down the old, spare the others.' Every day, Death sought them out and obeyed the law. One day, it entered a family and saw the old woman dandling a baby.
>
> 'Come!' said Death.
>
> 'Have pity!' the old woman answered. 'I'm still of use. Look!'
>
> 'Right' said Death. It went away and that night told God about it.
>
> 'You have disobeyed me,' said God. 'So become blind. Tomorrow when you work whoever you touch will die.'
>
> Since then people of all ages die.*

*Thomas, 1982:43

I have received a threatening letter. It does not involve unpaid bills, religion or obnoxious personal views. I am not even being berated as a once-loved, now-hated individual in the course of those marital shifts that seem to characterize our times. It is not from someone who knows me intimately nor someone to whom I am a mere generalized political target. It is not even from the government. And it comes in the form of a birthday card. It was sent to me – as it is every year on my birthday – by the man who sold me life insurance. On the front there is, as usual, a cuddly animal in some way representing thrift. This time it is a dormouse, cheek pouches bulging, stowing away nuts for the lean times ahead. A contact number is discreetly printed on the back. I can't even respond in kind. I don't know when his birthday is.

Muslims disdain life insurance because it is an impertinent betting against God, pitting human will and knowledge against divine omniscience and intention, the same argument used to condemn suicide. God alone properly controls life and death. Sir Edward Evans-Pritchard pointed out many years ago that one of the basic differences between cultures that invoke witchcraft explanations and those that do not is the point at which explanation is given up.* In the West, the cause of death is a general disease, or mere chance. Elsewhere, it may be necessary to fine tune the explanation. Why did this particular man die of that particular cause at that particular time? Factors we declare unknowable or within the domain of divinity. And we even reject statistical measures of probable mortality by clinging to the memory of Uncle George who smoked sixty a day till his nineties.

One of the commonest sources of ethnic friction in Singapore is gambling. The Malays, as Muslims, see it as the fast track to damnation. The Chinese have a reputation for betting on anything, the cries of birds, car numberplates, telephone numbers, worst of all in Malay eyes, they insist on doing it at funerals. Friends and relatives sit in front of the coffin gambling with great

*Evans-Pritchard, 1937

cries of loss or triumph. Malay complaints are met with the reply that gambling is an essential part of the funeral. If you ask about it, the Chinese mourners shrug and say, 'It passes the time' or 'We do it to make the ghost happy', 'It makes the dead rich' or 'Isn't all of life and death a gamble?' Educated Chinese slant their answers to exploit Western distinctions. 'It is not gambling,' they say, shocked. 'It is *ritual* gambling.' Is it always cards? you ask. What about mah-jong? 'Oh no, that would be too noisy.' But your informant has to shout for his answer to be heard because the card players are all screaming and outside a group of young men are climbing into a careering truck crashing cymbals together. 'The sounds of life,' they say. 'The dead like that.'

A similar story is told by the Balinese. They gamble with cards before a normal burial but every major ceremony of cremation, where the bodies are exhumed and burned, demands a cockfight. There are many aspects to a cockfight as Clifford Geertz has doggedly maintained.* Yet every fight has a winner and a loser, a survival and a death.

Every sudden fortune or misfortune offers the opportunity to show fortitude, gratitude or attitude but the best form of death in Bali is one where someone calmly announces and embraces the time of his own passing with total equanimity. Such deaths are very rare but it seems that at such harmonious cremations, the unpredictability of cockfights is not appropriate.

In many parts of the world, gambling is intimately associated with death for it speaks a language of skill and chance, unpredictability and destiny, personal hostility and solidarity, irrevocability and incremental disaster or 'sudden death'. You can break the rules but no one cheats death.

The ancient Egyptian board game of *snt* was a model for the confrontation with mortality itself. Wall paintings in tombs show a single human player opposing an invisible opponent, Death. The player progressed along a path like Monopoly and squares might be inscribed with instructions related to dying such as, 'You tread

*Geertz, 1975:15

221

the staircase of the souls of Heliopolis' or 'You shall ferry across the lake without wading.'

New Guinea Highlanders, looking at Western administrators, are impressed with the control that they expect to have over the world, the lack of unpredictability in their estimations. Often, after So-and-So has returned home, the Highlanders hear that he has died shortly afterwards. It is widely believed that a foreigner looks up the time of his own death in one of his many books of schedules and timetables and makes sure to return in good time to finish his own coffin.

But it is perhaps in South America that the link between death and gambling is closest. In Ecuador, men play a die game called *huairu* across the very body of the dead.* The bone die is unbalanced so that skill is involved in throwing and manipulating it and the biggest scores are achieved by making it stand upright against nature. The players are not close relatives of the dead and even disguise themselves but the result is held to rest upon the direct intervention of the deceased whose soul is contained in the die. So it becomes a means of divining his affections and – as at the Chinese wake – of creating an ambience of plenty that has implications for the future of all the survivors. The men actually gamble for the wealth of the dead that may be consumed in a feast on the spot. Those who score zero are punished by the winners by whipping or a blow to the head but their oppressors are just acting for the deceased whose spirit thus reduces random events to expressions of its last will and testament.

In our own culture, we relentlessly crank the handle of the genetic fruit machine and rail with equal piety against those who try to control the sex of offspring and those who *fail* to control the occasion of their births. We have experts, actuaries, who calculate the risk of death of different classes of humanity and bet against them in life insurance. As genetic profiling becomes more general, it becomes easier to predict not just when we will die – when our number will be up – but what we will die of. Disquiet

*Karsten, 1930

is spreading about how fine the mesh of classifications should be made, how the dice should be loaded against us in bets on our mortality, for no life insurance can mean no credit, no mortgage, no house, no social life. Worse, the less unpredictability there is in death, the more we are prisoners of a predetermined destiny, no longer free. Sociology has already paid the price of public hostility for wanting to put individuals in statistical cages and we teeter unhappily between too much certainty and too much contingency in death.

So the insurance man's birthday card is a reminder that I have been looked up and fitted into the actuarial tables and that the roulette wheel is still turning – though slowing – and the ball is waiting to drop into its statistically correct slot. It is an impoverished version of the Mesoamerican ball games, played in magnificent stone ball courts, where the match was between the living and the dead, re-enacting myths of annual, dynastic and cosmic renewal – but the game was rigged. The loser often lost his life and so, in human terms, death always won. Yet cosmically the issue was fudged. Death led to rebirth so that life was the final winner. In Mesoamerica, as with life insurance, the only way to really win is to lose – so that you never get to carry your winnings away from the table.

Bibliography

Abrahamsson, H., 'The Origin of Death', *Studia Ethnographica Upsaliensia* III, 1951

Adams, M., 'Style in Southeast Asian Materials Processing: Some Implications for Ritual and Art' in *Material Culture, Style, Organizationa and Dynamics of Technology*, ed. by H. Lechtmann and R. Merrill, Proc. American Ethnological Society, 1977

Ardener, E., 'Witchcraft, Economics and the Continuity of Belief' in *Witchcraft Accusations and Confessions*, ed. by M. Douglas, London: Tavistock, 1970

Arens, W., *The Man-Eating Myth*, Oxford University Press: New York, 1979

Arhem, K., 'Milk, Meat and Blood: Diet as a Cultural Code among the Pastoral Maasai' in *The Creative Communion*, ed. by A. Jacobson-Widding and W. van Beek, Uppsala, 1988

Aries, P., *The Hour of Our Death*, London: Allen Lane, 1981

Asquith, P., 'The Monkey Memorial Service of Japanese Primatologists', Royal Anthropological Institute Newsletter, No. 54, 1983

Astuti, R., 'Invisible Objects' *Res* 25:111–22, 1994

Aubrey, J., *Remains of Gentilisme and Judaisme*, London: Stachell, Peyton and Co., 1881

225

Bagliani, A., 'Demembrement et integrite du corps au XIIIe siecle', *Terrain*, 18:26–32, 1992

Baumann, Z., *Mortality, Immortality and Other Life Strategies*, Oxford: Polity, 1993

Binns, C., 'The changing face of power: revolution and accommodation in the development of the Soviet ceremonial system I, *Man*, 14 (4): 585–606, 1979

— 'II', *Man*, 15 (1): 170–87, 1980

Bloch, M., 'Tombs and States' in *Mortality and Immortality*, ed. by S. Humphries and H. King, London: Academic Press, 1981

— 'Almost eating the ancestors', *Man*, 20 (4): 631–46, 1982

Bloch, M. and Parry, J., *Death and the Regeneration of Life*, Cambridge University Press, 1982

Boddy, J., 'The Body as Oasis', *American Ethnologist*, 9 (4): 682–98, 1982

Bundy, R., 'Folktales from Liberia', *Journal of American Folklore*, 31, 1919

Carneiro da Cunha, M., 'Eschatology among the Kraho: reflection upon society, free field of fabulation' in *Mortality and Immortality*, London: Academic Press, 1981

Casaverde, 'El mundo sobrenatural en una comunidad', *Allpanchis*, (3): 121–244, 1970

Corlin, C., 'The Journey Through the Bardo' in *On the Meaning of Death*, ed. by S. Cederroth et al., Uppsala Studies in Cultural Anthropology 8, Uppsala, 1988

Davis, W., *Passage of Darkness*, Chapel Hill and London: University of North Carolina Press, 1988

Descola, P., *Les Lances du Crepuscule*, Paris: Plon, 1994

Dover, K., *Greek Homosexuality*, New York: Vintage, 1978

Dubois, H.-M., 'Monographie des Betsileo', *Travaux et Memoires de L'Institute d'Ethnologie*, XXXIV, 1938

Eicher, J. and Erekosima, T., 'Kalabari Funerals: Celebration and Display', *African Arts*, XXI (1): 38–45, 1987

Evans-Pritchard, E., *Witchcraft, oracles and magic among the Azande*, Oxford: Clarendon, 1937

Firth, R., *We, the Tikopia*, London: George Allen and Unwin, 1936

Fortes, M., *The Web of Kinship Among the Tallensi*, London: OUP, 1949

Fortune, R., *Sorcerers of Dobu*, London: Routledge, 1932

Fox, J., 'On Bad Death and the Left Hand: A Study of Rotinese Symbolic Inversions', in *Right and Left*, ed. by R. Needham, Chicago and London: University of Chicago Press, 1973

— 'Sister's Child as Plant' in *Rethinking Kinship and Marriage*, ed. by R. Needham, London: Tavistock, 1983

Freedman, M., *The Study of Chinese Society*, Stanford: Stanford University Press, 1979

Freeman, J., *Report on the Iban*, London: Athlone, 1970

Geary, P., 'Sacred commodities: the circulation of medieval relics' in *The Social Life of Things*, ed. by A. Appadurai, Cambridge University Press, 1988

Geertz, C., *The Interpretation of Cultures*, London: Hutchinson, 1975

Gittinger, M., *Splendid Symbols*, Singapore: Oxford University Press, 1985

— *To Speak With Cloth*, Los Angeles: Museum of Cultural History, 1989

Gittings, C., *Death, Burial and the Individual in Early Modern England*, London: Routledge, 1988

Goody, J., *Death, Property and the Ancestors*, London: Tavistock, 1962

Gose, P., 'Sacrifice and the commodity form in the Andes', *Man*, 21 (2): 293–310, 1986

Gossen, G., *Chamulas in the World of the Sun*, Cambridge: Harvard University Press, 1974

Griaule, M., *Dieux d'eau: Entretiens avec Ogotemmeli*, Paris: Editions du Chene, 1948

Gutmann, B., *Dichten und Denken der Dschagganeger*, Leipzig: Evang.–Luth. Mission, 1909

Habenstein, R. and Lamers, W., *Funeral Customs the World Over*, Milwaukee, 1960

Harrison, S., *The Mask of War*, Manchester and New York, Manchester University Press, 1993

Heritier-Izard, F., 'Univers Feminin et destin individuel chez les Samo' in *La Notion de la Personne en Afrique Noire*, Paris: Centre National de Recherches Scientifiques, 1983

Hertz, R., 'A contribution to the collective representation of death' in *Death and the Right Hand*, Glencoe: Free Press, 1960 (orig. 1907)

de Heusch, L., 'Heat, Physiology and Cosmogeny: *Rites de Passage* among the Thonga' in *Explorations in African Systems of Thought*, ed. by I. Karp and C. Bird, Bloomington, Indiana University Press, 1980

Hobart, M., 'The elixir of mortality: Towards a Balinese economy of Death', Unpublished, 1987

Hope, W., 'On the Funeral Effigies of the Kings and Queens of England with special reference to those in the Abbey Church of Westminster', *Archaeologia*, LX (2): 511–64, 1903

Hoskins, J., 'So My Name Shall Live: Stone-Dragging and Grave-Building in Kodi, West Sumba' *Bijdragen to de Taal-, Land- en Volkenkunde*, 142 (1): 31–51, 1986

Huntington, R., and Metcalf, P., *Celebrations of Death*, Cambridge University Press, 1980

Irving, W., 'Rural Funerals' in *The Sketchbook of George Crayon*, London, 1820

Jacobson-Widding, A., 'The Red Corpse, or the Ambiguous Father, *Ethnos*, 45 (3–4): 202–10, 1980

— 'The Fertility of Incest' in *The Creative Communion* ed. by A. Jacobson-Widding and W. van Beek, Uppsala Studies in Cultural Anthropology 15, Uppsala, 1990

Jacobson-Widding, A., and van Beek, W., *The Creative Communion*, Uppsala Studies in Cultural Anthropology 15.

Jensen, E., *The Iban and Their Religion*, Oxford: Clarendon Press, 1974

Junod, H., 'Les conceptions physiologiques des bantous sud-africains et leurs tabous', *Revue d'Ethnographie et de Sociologie*, 1: 126–69, 1910

Kan, S., *Symbolic Immortality*, Washington and London: Smithsonian Institution Press, 1989

Kantorowicz, E., *The King's Two Bodies*, Princeton University Press, 1957

Karsten, R., 'Ceremonial games of the South American Indians', *Commentationes Humanarum Letterarum*, III(2), Societas Scientiarum Fennica, 1930

Kearl, M., *Endings*, New York and Oxford: Oxford University Press, 1989

Kelly, R., 'Witchcraft and sexual relations: an exploration in the social and semantic implications of the structure of belief' in *Men and Women in the New Guinea Highlands*, ed. by P. Brown and G. Buchbinder, Washington D.C.: American Anthropological Association, 1976

Koch, E., 'Death and Justice', *New Republic*, 15 April: 12–15, 1985

Kohl, J., *Kitchi-Gami*, St. Paul: Minnesota Historical Society Press, 1985

Kopytoff, I., 'Ancestors as Elders in Africa' *Man*, 41 (2): 129–42, 1971

Leach, E., *Rethinking Anthropology*, London: Athlone, 1961

— *Culture and Communication*, Cambridge University Press, 1976

Le Moal, G., *Les Bobo. Nature et fonction des masques*, Paris: Organisation de Recherches Scientifiques et Techniques d'outre Mer, 1980

Levi-Strauss, C., *The Elementary Structures of Kinship*, London: Eyre and Spottiswoode, 1969

— *The Raw and the Cooked*, London: Cape, 1970

Litten, J., *The English Way of Death*, London: Robert Hale, 1992

Llewellyn, N., *The Art of Death*, London: Redaktion, 1991

Mack, J., *Madagascar: Island of the Ancestors*, London: British Museum Press, 1986

Mackinnon, S., 'Flags and Half-Moons: Tanimbarese Textiles in an 'Engendered' System of Valuables' in *To Speak with Cloth*, ed. by M. Gittinger, Los Angeles: Museum of Cultural History, 1989

Malinowski, B., 'Baloma: the spirits of the dead in the Trobriand Islands', *Journal of the Royal Anthropological Institute*, 45, 1916
— *The sexual life of savages in north-western Melanesia*, New York: Meridian, 1929
Mansfeld, A., *Urwald-Dokumente*, Berlin: Mansfeld, 1908
Marcus, D., *Dead Elvis*, London: Harmondsworth, 1992
Martin, E., 'Gender and Ideological Differences in Representations of Life and Death' in *Death Ritual in Late Imperial and Modern China*, ed. by J. Watson and E. Rawski, Berkeley and Los Angeles: University of California Press, 1988
Meunier, J., *Voyages sans alibi*, Paris: Flammarion, 1994
Morley, J., *Death, Heaven and the Victorians*, London, 1971
Mosko, M., *Quadripartite Structures: categories, relations and homologies in Bush Mekeo culture*, Cambridge University Press, 1985
Muensterberger, W., *Collecting*, Princeton University Press, 1994
Olson, R., *Social Life and Social Structure of the Tlingit Indians in Alaska*, University of California Anthrop. Records 26, 1967
Overing, J., 'Death and the loss of civilized predation among the Piaroa', *L'Homme*: 126–8, 1993
Parry, J., 'Sacrificial death and the necrophagous ascetic' in *Death and the Regeneration of Life*, ed. by M. Bloch and J. Parry, Cambridge University Press, 1982
Paulme, D., *La mere devorante*, Paris: Gallimard, 1978
Plowden, E., *Commentaries on Reports*, London, 1816
Puckle, B., *Funeral Customs, Their Origin and Development*, London, 1926
Radcliffe-Brown, A., *The Andaman Islanders*, Cambridge University Press, 1933
Rattray, R., *Religion and Art in Ashanti*, Oxford: Clarendon Press, 1927
Rein-Wuhrmann, A., *Mein Bamunvolk im Grasland von Kamerun*, Stuttgart, 1925
Rivers, W., *Psychology and Ethnology*, London: Kegan Paul, 1926
Rubin, A., *Marks of Civilization*, Los Angeles: Museum of Cultural History, 1988

Sahlins, M., 'Raw Women, Cooked Men, and Other "Great Things" of the Fiji Islands' in *The Ethnography of Cannibalism*, ed. by P. Brown and D. Tuzin: Washington DC, 1983

Sanday, P., *Divine Hunger*, Cambridge University Press, 1986

Scheff, T., 'The Distancing of Emotion in Ritual', *Current Anthropology*, 18 (3): 483–505, 1977

Schmitt, J.C., *The holy greyhound*, Cambridge University Press, 1988

Siegel, J., 'Images and Odors in Javanese Practices Surrounding Death', *Indonesia*, 36: 1–14, 1983

Spencer, B., and Gillen, F., *Across Australia*, London: Macmillan, 1912

Sterner, J., 'Who is Signalling Whom? Ceramic Style, Ethnicity and Taxonomy among the Sirak Bulahay, *Antiquity*, 63: 451–9, 1989

Stone, L., *The Family, Sex and Marriage in England 1500–1800*, London: Weidenfeld and Nicolson, 1977

Strathern, A., *The Rope of Moka*, Cambridge University Press, 1971

Strong, S., *Shining Path*: Fontana, 1993

Tambiah, S., 'On flying witches and flying canoes: the coding of male and female values' in *The Kula*, ed. by J. Leach and E. Leach, Cambridge University Press, 1983

Taylor, C., 'Remembering to forget: identity, mourning and memory among the Jivaro' *Man*, 28 (4): 653–78, 1993

Thomas, L.-V., *La Mort Africaine*, Paris: Payot, 1982

Thompson, M., *Rubbish Theory*, Oxford University Press, 1976

Thompson, S. 'Death, Food and Fertility' in *Death Ritual in Late Imperial and Modern China*, ed. by J. Watson and E. Rawski, Berkeley and Los Angeles: University of California Press, 1988

Topley, M., 'Chinese Rites for the Repose of the Soul', *Journal of the Malayan Branch of the Royal Malaysian Society*, Vol. 25, pt. 1: 148–59, 1952

Valch, J., *The Afro-American Tradition in Decorative Arts*, Cleveland, 1978 van Baal, J., *Dema*, The Hague: Nijhoff, 1966

van Gennep, A., *The Rites of Passage*, London: Routledge, 1977 (orig. 1909)

Wakeman, F., 'Mao's Remains' in *Death Ritual in Late Imperial and Modern China*, ed. by J. Watson and E. Rawski, Berkeley and Los Angeles: University of California Press, 1988

Watson, J., 'Of Flesh and Bones: The Management of Death Pollution in Cantonese Society' in *Death and the Regeneration of Life*, ed. by M. Bloch and J. Parry, Cambridge University Press, 1982

Watson, J., and Rawski, E., *Death Ritual in Late Imperial and Modern China*, Berkeley and Los Angeles: University of California Press, 1988

Weiner, A., *Women of Value, Men of Renown*, Austin and London: University of Texas Press, 1976

Wilson, G., 'Nyakyusa Conventions of Burial', *Bantu Studies*, 1939

Windsor, J. 'Identity Parades' in *The Cultures of Collecting*, ed. by J. Elsner and R. Cardinal, London: Reaktion, 1994

Yoshida, K., 'Masks and Transformation among the Chewa of Eastern Zambia', *Senri Ethnological Studies*, No. 31, Africa 4: 203–74, 1992

Zegwaard, G., 'Headhunting Practices of the Asmat of Netherlands New Guinea' in *Peoples and Cultures of the Pacific*, ed. by A. Vayda, New York: Natural History Press, 1968

Index

233

239